Fire Lilies

Life Out of the Ashes

By Kim Krenik

Line Editor: Dr. Marian at First Editing
2nd Editor: Linda Heard
3rd Editor: Amanda Langston

To
Nathan, Keira, Lucas, and Bethany.
My Fantastic Four.

&

Mom.
The Greatest Mom of the 20th and 21st Centuries.

XOXO

Table of Contents

Acknowledgments

Allison Simpson, I would not have been propelled forward to finish this book and share it with anyone if it weren't for you. I thank you, your Mom and your cousin for requesting to use the book (even while it was still being written) and for taking on the challenges. You were the first "testers!"

Rob Krenik, my sweet man, my rock who stays by my side through the lows and to the mountaintops.

Rebecca, thank you for your friendship and your valuable input. I can't wait to do the same for you once you finish your first book ! (Hint)

Heather, your constructive feedback and insights were amazing! Thank you for standing with me through life, my friend.

My prayer pal and kindred spirit, Kelby Bruno.

All of those who have faithfully prayed for me throughout the years, thank you. Your prayers go up to heaven as a sweet, fragrant offering.

Teresa Sylvester, what a gift you have been given as an artist. Your cover design motivated me to finish the book!

Debbie Alsdorf, you poured into me when I was in my twenties, and to this day I know I can call for wise counsel and you will give it faithfully. I will always look to you as my mentor and friend.

Bree Noble, your mentorship through the Female Musician's Academy is priceless.

To my Calvary Chapel Tracy family: So thankful to "do life" with you, a wellspring in this valley.

To my amazing editor, Amanda Langston, *thank you*!

Jeannine, Pam, Angela and Madi: Thank you for pouring yourself out into the ladies at Calvary Chapel Tracy and for being prayerful and supportive women in my life.

Thanks to the speakers who impacted me at the Calvary Chapel Pastor's Wives' Conference. Lenya Heitzig, in particular, shared a session on "Spiritual Warfare," which led me to write the chapter and the song, "Warrior Pose." June Hesterly shared a humorous and truthful session on "Waiting on the Lord" with wonderful examples of how NOT to wait!

Each of you is more spectacular, and more precious to Your Maker than fire lilies.

Foreword by Debbie Alsdorf

We all grow up wanting a beautiful life. But before long we find out that life is hard. Those hard seasons are what draw many of us to the Christian faith. From that point on, it is easy to hope that Jesus would sprinkle some kind of magic on our lives, so we can live happily ever after. What we dared to hope for is not reality, and so once again we realize that life is hard—even as a Christian.

For the past 30 years, I have had the joy of ministering to women. Women are complicated. But, women are the heartbeat of the homes, churches, and community. If the heart is not beating to the proper rhythm, things go awry. There is nothing so sad as a woman whose spiritual heart has lost its beat due to discouragement and defeat. Too many times to count, I have come across women who no longer dare to hope. They have been disappointed by people, circumstances, and yes, even God. It's quite sad, and I always wonder if what we expected from God was off from the beginning. It wasn't Jesus who promised the perfect life—truth is He said we would have troubles but that He has already overcome them. I guess we can say that faith makes all things possible—not easy.

I have had hard days, hard months, and hard years. But, what I have come to know is that Jesus does indeed work within the hard-to-change me and bring beauty out of life's ashes. Facing life as it is, not as I wished it would be, is what this Fire Lilies Bible Study is all about—taking our story and realizing that God is in each and every piece of it, the triumphs as well as the tears.

In the Fire Lilies Bible Study you will look at Scripture and get a clearer view of the grand story that we are all privileged to be a part of. That story includes things that might be hard, but God will always prove faithful. We fail—He does not. And even in our times of failing, His love reaches out to us.

In this study Kim Krenik gives us tools to push us toward the truth of God's Word, as well as fun and refreshing spiritual exercises. Together these things will bring a woman's heart nearer to the heartbeat of a God who is faithful to her, always.

I am blessed by Kim Krenik's life. I have known her since she was in her twenties. I have watched her go through some of what she speaks of in this book. To see the faithfulness of God in her life encourages me. To see her faithfulness to God's call brings me great joy. For I know there is nothing that can separate us from God's love, and that has played out in her own life.

May this study cause you to truly change, and may you carry the truth with you into a life that is a demonstration of how Jesus brings beauty out of ashes.

Debbie Alsdorf
www.design4living.org

Introduction

Isaiah 61:3 KJV
"To appoint unto them that mourn in Zion, to give unto them beauty for ashes, the oil of joy for mourning, the garment of praise for the spirit of heaviness, that they might be called trees of righteousness, the planting of the Lord, that He might be glorified."

The date was August 26, 2010. The story I read in my Springs in the Valley devotional, by Mrs. Charles Cowman, was about the fire lily. Have you heard of this rare and beautiful flower? Before I read the devotional that morning, this little creation was unknown to me.

In South Africa, the grassland regions frequently have grass fires when the dry season hits. After the fire, there is nothing but a black patch of dirt left. Then after some time, radiant splashes of red spring up and cover the blackened ground—flowers known as fire lilies. Interestingly, these flowers, also known as the George Lily or the Scarborough Lily, grow and bloom best after being dormant for some time.

The Great Designer doesn't create anything by accident. The fire lilies are a glimpse of the beautiful life that you and I can know, even after times when we have suffered loss, death or barrenness, or after seasons where we have experienced a sort of "dormancy."

I relate to the pain of losing someone. I have said goodbye to many who have passed on, including my beloved Grandmother, who I called Nar-Nar, as well as several friends and church members over the years. One year I went to five funerals within a three-month time period. I have lost a few friends to suicide, and all of those friends were believers. I have grieved and continue to grieve with dear friends as they buried their infants.

Another type of loss, which doesn't seem as serious, yet if we are honest it can take a serious toll on us, is the loss of a dream or the season of waiting for a dream to be fulfilled. As a single woman, I remember feeling like it was taking forever to find a husband. Then I married my husband at 26 years old, but I had to wait another six years before I could become pregnant.

I also had a different dream for my life and the way I thought it would be one day. I wanted to be a "musicianary" (traveling and making music for God's glory). But I married a guy who decided to become a pastor and plant a church in one of my least favorite areas in California: the Central Valley.

Growing up, I used to drive through this valley of pesticides, hay and dust on my way to visit my cousins in Modesto and suffer severe allergy attacks. I swore this would be the last place I would live when I grew up.

I have gone through seasons where I have felt like God had forgotten me, abandoned me. I have been deceived at times by believing that He loved His other kids more than He loved me. I have seen pain and difficulty in my marriage, miscarried two babies, and suffered through illnesses (both my own and my husband's). The church that my husband pastors has also been through quite a lot, and the pressure of being a pastor's wife and in a sort of a fishbowl has been the cause of many gray hairs and at times triggered increased weight gain! Ugh.

How about you? I bet you have a few things to recount. The longer we live on this planet, the more likely we are to have some stories to tell!

The inspiration came for this book after hearing a few different women teach at a Calvary Chapel Pastor's Wives conference in 2010. During that time when my soul was searching and thirsty for answers, I began waking up before the kids so I could have quiet time to read the Bible and my devotionals, and then I would write down the things God was revealing to me. I did not know at the time I would ever share my writing with anyone else.

When God teaches us and reveals to us amazing truth, we are set free, aren't we? Well, as that began to happen to me, I couldn't help but want to share with people who needed encouragement. Somewhere along the way, I felt that I needed to put my own journaling into a book where others might also be blessed.

Come Alive Dry Bones!

Ezekiel 37 is a story about how God takes a valley of dry bones and causes flesh and muscles to form over them. God uses his servant, a man named Ezekiel, to speak words of life into the bones. Ezekiel watches in amazement as the bones rise up out of the ground as the muscles and skin begin to form. Then God tells Ezekiel to speak to the four winds, and God uses the winds to breathe life back into those dead bodies. Does that sound like a fantasy film or what? Read this story yourself in Ezekiel 37. It's in the Bible, I'm not joshin' ya!

Are you like the fire lily? Have you experienced loss? The severing of a relationship? The death of a dream? A barren womb? You may feel the locusts have eaten away years of your life. You may feel you have no hope left. But as long as there is breath in you, there is still hope that all the death and pain can be transformed into glorious, radiant beauty.

When the concept of this book first came into my mind, I saw a picture of myself alone on the hill, a single fire lily. But a few months later, I had a new picture enter my head. Many fire were lilies springing up everywhere, covering the hills of ash in blazing colors. That was when I realized that this was not just a message for me. He wanted me to share with each of you.

God sees you as one of His beautiful creations. Perhaps you do not see yourself this way right now, but as you read on, my hope for you is that new life will spring up inside you and embrace the abundant life you are meant to enjoy, that you may live out the purpose you have been created to fulfill.

How to Use This Book

It is one thing to read a book; it is another thing for a book to actually lead you to make a change. My hope is that God would use this book to bring about change in your life. Of course, this can't happen without willingness on your part. But if change is what you are reaching for, I encourage you to take on each challenge in the book. Accountability is the key to truly make changes happen in our lives. Ask a friend or a group of friends to meet. If getting together with people doesn't work, try connecting with them through social media regularly to discuss chapters.

This book is best used for two or more people, since the challenges before you will most likely become a reality when you have a friend or group of friends to do them with and discuss things over. Each challenge can be done each time you meet, or break it down into your own schedule that works best for you. If you are the creative type of group leader, feel free to tweak the challenges to fit your group.

My "tester" group has suggested to me that they have needed extra time to sit with certain challenges. For example, Challenge 1 could easily be broken up into a four-week study in Psalm 139. How long you take going through chapters really will depend upon you, your group, and their needs.

This book involves looking up references in scripture verses from the Old and New Testaments of the Bible. If you don't have one, the New International Version is easy to understand.

These days you can look all the scripture references up on your computers and smart phones if you prefer. I personally am "old school" and like the real feel of turning pages. I recommend purchasing a notebook for your challenge questions. In this book, all of my scripture references are from the King James Version. You can use biblegateway.com to read any translation you wish.

Bible Study & Small Group Leaders

There is not one perfect way to facilitate a small group. Everyone is unique and will have their own "style," which I feel is actually rather wonderful.

However, for those leaders who are new at facilitating, and would like a little help with preparing, here are a couple of examples of how to hostess a group:

Model 1:

This is a model I have seen used in the past, and I used it myself when I was leading our women's ministry. It works well.

1. Set out some snacks, waters, coffee. Pass around a sheet to divvy up the weeks and have a different person bring the snack each time you meet.
2. Ask everyone to take a seat, and say a prayer to invite the Holy Spirit to be in the midst of your time.
3. Sing a few worship songs or old hymns together.
4. Invite the ladies to share freely when you start going through the challenge questions. Also, give the ladies freedom to pass if they are not comfortable sharing.
5. Keep four simple rules: 1. Be good listeners, rather than "fixers." 2. No spouse bashing. 3. No people bashing. 4. No church bashing.

Model 2:

This model is what our church's women's leader did when she went through this book with our ladies. It worked very well. I asked Jeannine to share with you all how she leads her morning study. Here is what she wrote:

"We took our time through each chapter. We read the scripture aloud. Then I would give the ladies the opportunity to share from their hearts or from their journals, discussing previous questions in the book. After that we opened up for discussion. For example, one day we spent 45 minutes discussing real love (1 Cor. 13).

Another day, we spent a lengthy time in prayer. I have been encouraging the ladies to take your advice in the book and to 'steep' in what God wants to teach them. My advice at this point is to take it as slowly as the particular group wants."

If you decide to lead a group, I encourage you to pray and ask God to lead you as you lead others. Take a minute to pray for your group members daily. If you have time, give them a call in the middle of the week to check in with them and offer to pray for them.

Encourage each person to use their gifts and to do things they enjoy to serve in the group. If you have a few people who love to cook or bake, ask them to use their gift to serve the group. If there are one or more ladies who like to make phone calls and write letters, and they have the time to do so, ask them to touch base mid-week with the group members. This takes the burden off of one person and everyone is blessed if they are serving by using the gift God gave them.

1
The Power of Story: Your Story

We often discount our own lives, our own stories. We believe they don't really matter in the larger span of world history. But imagine if the Jews decided to eliminate some of the stories from our Bible history. What if Rahab was never mentioned? Or Miriam? What if Hosea's or Jonah's stories were never told?

"Yet who knows whether you have come to the kingdom for such a time as this?"
Esther 4:14 KJV

Your story does matter. Someone out there does need to hear it. The greatest victory our enemy has over us is convincing us our lives have no purpose and no meaning. We will act according to our beliefs.

God doesn't intend for you to live vicariously through a fantasy video game, a film you love, or another person's life. He has purpose and adventure awaiting you. The question is: will you choose to step out of your comfortable little living room and plunge into the unknown with Him as your leader? If you long to live a full, abundant life, it is possible!

For many years, I have prayed and asked God to open the doors for me to tour again. In the past, this was an idea that would have been too difficult, with the age of my kids. But life has its seasons, babies become children, teens, and before long they are adults!

Our kids are growing quickly, and at the age where they can learn some skills on a working road trip. The very best way to sell CDs and books is to take them to the people. As long as I have waited to tour again, I have to admit, the reality of doing it is a bit frightful.

Fear—A Serious Killjoy

Fear can really mess with your mind. Its punch has the potential to paralyze.

Fear has held me back from asking and knocking on doors for a great portion of my life. The greatest fear of all: "What will that person think of me if I …?"

You fill in the blank. For me: "…if I pitch my song to them", "…if I try to be a Mom and a working musician", "…if I share what God is telling me to share with them"?

Fear caused me to freeze as a writer for a season. I would often look at other people writing books and think, "What will they say about me if I write a book? They are way better at this than I am." Comparison always finds its roots in fear.

Then about six months later, after a long season of not writing and ignoring the little voice in my head, I picked up a Worship Leader magazine that has been in my bathroom since 2009. (ahem...don't go there, those of you who share my warped sense of humor.) On the cover it said, "Stories." As I read article after article, I absorbed each word like dry soil taking in water. My convictions about touring and writing were at the forefront of my mind once again. Everything inside me resonated that I was ignoring my calling.

There are seasons and valid reasons for us to put our passions on hold. When my children were infants, it was not the best timing. I had been sitting on the sidelines for so long that when I heard the Coach say, "Okay, time to get in on the action," I was feeling content just to watch the other players and root them on! Meanwhile I was getting lazier and chubbier on my popcorn and ice cream. I had to make the decision, am I going to stay in the dugout, or am I going to push myself to get back into the game?

Fist Fights with Fear

A war had broken out between Faith and Fear inside of me, and Fear's fists had been pounding down Faith without ceasing. Faith was having trouble catching her breath. Would I let Fear keep bullying Faith like that?

Or would I take some action and tell Fear where to go? So I took a little step with Faith. I contacted another songwriter who I respect and who I knew would challenge me, and I set up a collaboration date with her. We both share a heart to encourage other writers so we decided to host a songwriter's conference.

The writers who came were all gifted, and I was blessed to meet a group of worship leaders who are from various churches in Northern California.

Taking one baby step away from fear was a step in the right direction.

Did I start back on writing right away? Yeah...uh...no. I didn't. But the thought was back in my head that I needed to get alone with God and keep writing. Taking one baby step away from fear was a step in the right direction. No, it wasn't a LEAP of faith, but at least it was something.

Sometimes people like me need a little shove to get where we need to go. I would say I got a good push one summer at the annual Share the Scoop Women's Conference in Tracy. The speaker was Kathi Lipp, and her topic was: Stories.

One particular thing she shared felt like an arrow piercing my heart. She said many of us don't share our stories because we are perfectionists. We want the outcome of our story to be the perfect ending. Most of all, we want to come out looking good in the end.

However, as she pointed out, if we are more concerned about ourselves looking good, we can often forget that the reason we are meant to share our story is so God will look good. It would be better to tell the truth about what a mess WE made, and tell about all that GOD has done. Throughout the Bible we see this modeled for us. What if the scribes only chose to wait for happy, perfect endings that made the Jews look good? We would have some very different accounts given in the Greatest Story Ever Told.

Everything she shared echoed what I already knew in my head and my spirit. It was a loud trumpet call for me to sit down already and get busy.

Did I start writing then? Aaaargh... NO! (I know you Type A go-getters want to choke me right now. I am the baby of a family of seven children. That's my excuse.)

At this point the kids were back in school and I had no excuses left, except that I was saying yes to many things that were thrust upon me that I didn't necessarily want to do or feel I should do, and I needed to wo-man up and say, "NO."

I asked a friend to pray for me in this area. During that conversation, it came up that she wanted me to go down to her church in Redondo Beach and perform my song, "The Lion." She had tried to get me to come down in the past, but it was never the right time. This time I felt like I needed to make it happen.

This time, instead of caving to the negative thoughts, I decided to follow that still, small voice, which urged me to go.

"After the earthquake came a fire, but the Lord was not in the fire. And after the fire a still small voice."
1 Kings 19:12 KJV

Kelby and I would be leading three of their services in worship, and I felt so incredibly weak and unfit for the task. But I sensed God really wanted to love on this church. So off we went, driving six hours to simply sing some songs and play the piano. I had negative thoughts like, "Why are we driving all the way down there for such a short weekend? What a waste of gas," going through my head on the drive down. But I felt like I needed to go. This time, instead of caving to the negative thoughts, I decided to follow that still, small voice, which still urged me to go.

I was amazed at how God used us and poured himself out at all three services. The people were so hungry to worship God. The worship team I played with was a blessing to work with. All my CDs all sold out at the first service, which was something I really did not expect.

Kelby's husband was also a blessing to us by watching my two girls Saturday and Sunday (bless his manly heart, Chris Bruno is a Texan and 100 percent man's man).

Then he washed my scarily and insanely dirty van inside and out before we drove home. God only knows the moldy, disgusting things he might have found. He was Jesus' hands and feet to us.

God's people were really behaving like God's people that weekend. I think they deserve a shout-out because that kind of Christianity is not the norm of what we see today, is it? When I see people act like Jesus, it gives me a glimpse into Heaven, and it gives me hope that life doesn't have to be all black roses. There are sweet, fragrant blossoms on this earth! Let us all recognize them and cherish them when they are thrown our way.

God's people were really behaving like God's people that weekend... I think they deserve a shout-out.

What did this show me, this trip to Redondo Beach? For one thing, I realized that it was possible to tour with the kids. I saw how God could orchestrate everything down to the tiniest detail. I realized that God can do amazing things when we obey His call on our lives.

That weekend was like the final trumpet call that awakened me to write again. I started waking extra early to write, once again. I took the next step.

Another Step into Your Story

My friends, along this journey we call life, we will probably lose some battles. We are going to experience loss and setbacks. The rain falls on both the wicked and the good. This can be discouraging. Discouragement will paralyze us if we allow it to.

The worst thing we can do is stop walking. The best thing we can do is start each day ready to listen to God. Then we can follow His lead and take each step, one at a time. In the midst of pain and loss, keep sharing the stories of God's amazing love and redemption in your life. Whether that means writing a book, a song, a blog on the Internet, sharing over coffee with a friend. There are many practical ways to shine your light.

Fire Lily

by Kim Krenik

Once there was a palace here
All I've built has been torn down
All my dreams have been stolen
Every stem burnt to the ground

Then you gently begin to breathe new life in me again

CHORUS
I surrender, I let go now
I am leaving the past behind
Resurrected out of ashes
Rediscovering the joy of life
Just like the fire lily lily lily oh oh
Like the fire lily lily lily oh oh

Then you gently begin to breathe new life in me again
And I know I'm loved, And I know I'm held
In the grip of Your Hand

1 Action Challenges

READ Psalm 139 in the morning before you start your day and at night just before you go to sleep every day this week

JOURNAL

1. Ps. 139: What does this passage say about what the Lord has done? Write any revelations that you get in your journal as you spend time reflecting.

2. Verses 7-12.
When you are afraid, how do these verses directly oppose your fears?

3. Verses 13 - 16:
Do you ever struggle with your body image?
Most of us don't look like airbrushed models. We can't possibly compare to the perfection we see in magazines and films. Psalm 139:13-16 is God's love letter to you, His creation. He formed you in the womb. Do you believe that? Do you believe you were made in His image?

I don't know about you, but I have had my share of days where I want to smash my mirror or discover a quick-fix diet. Psalm 139 is God talking directly to you and to me! If you struggle with self-image, embrace these verses. Be like a tealeaf in boiled water and steep. One day you're going to be a fine cup of tea. But first you have to steep a while.

4. Verses 17-18
Were you aware that God thinks about you? His thoughts about you are precious. Do you have a person who you think precious thoughts about? Write down those wonderful thoughts you have.
Imagine, God thinks this way about you. Let His love fall upon you now.

5. Sing a song! Why? Why are there verses in the Bible commanding us to sing and shout and make a joyful noise unto our Maker? Singing helps to unite your thoughts with your heart. You will find freedom as you allow your voice to sing, or even shout out the words of a Bible verse or worship song.

6. Write down your thoughts. Sit and ponder His love as long as you are able to. Perhaps you will write in your journal or write a prayer as a song and sing it to God. Know that He is all ears; He loves this time you spend with Him.

7. Read Verses 19-22

These verses almost seem out of place at first. The Psalmist has written the truth about God: who God is, what He has done, how He loves us is all accounted for in Psalm 139.

But there is also evil in this world, isn't there? As we worship our one true God, evil is always trying to invade our thoughts, trying to mess with our minds and keep us from worshiping God in spirit and in truth. The psalmist writes that indeed we should hate evil.

Along with hating evil, we need to be cleansed from hating people. Jesus told us to love our enemies. This is not a contradiction to the verses in Psalm 139. The Psalmist is writing his own thoughts about evil, but then he quickly asks God to do what?

8. Read Psalm 139: 23-24
Take the time now to allow God to search your heart, to test you, to reveal to you any ways you have offended Him. Write down the things God is showing you about Himself and write down the things you want him to free you from.

9. Share your insights and prayer requests with a friend or a group of friends who can pray for you and hold you accountable to the actions or habits you wish to see God change in you.

2

Well, I Never!

A person who is much loved, loves much
A person who is much forgiven, forgives much

A few years ago, a family member who was single brought a date with him to a family gathering. She was a perfect example of why we should not judge a book by its cover.

A couple of the women of the family commented on her attire, saying that she looked like a hooker. True, she was exposing a good amount of cleavage and she was far from conservatively dressed. She had a Bette Midler figure. Sometime that day when the guest was outside and a few of us were standing in the kitchen, someone commented, "She certainly isn't the type you would bring to church."

I thought to myself and even said out loud, "Actually she is definitely the type to bring to church. Look at who Jesus chose to spend time with: the hookers, the drunks. He was a friend to sinners." The person laughed and replied, "Well, maybe your church would be okay."

And thank God for that. I mean, I have to show up every week. I hope other sinners will feel welcome there! Later that day, I had the opportunity to chat with this lady a bit and found her to be thoughtful and intelligent.

She shared with me that she had a handicapped son who had some speech development issues, and I was empathetic as my four year old was going to be getting speech therapy.

In fact, after chatting with this woman even further, I found out she was a churchgoer. She seemed to have a good grasp on what the Bible taught.
She mentioned her struggle with feeling judged at a couple of churches, but she had found one she really liked. She spoke of Jesus with adoration, as if she probably knew Him well.

She could certainly have been more aware of her neckline and tried to find a shirt that revealed less cleavage. That would have been the best choice, yes. The thing is, not everyone grows up in church and gets the dress code memos. We all come from different backgrounds, and the reality of today's culture is that most of us weren't raised in church. Should we judge someone for what they don't know?

If an attractive woman (or young girl) walks into church inappropriately dressed, what would your first thought be? "Well, what a little tramp! Coming in here causing my husband and sons to stumble!" or "Oh that poor girl. Her Mama didn't teach her about modesty, did she? Well, I'll just go let the poor dear thing know she is welcome here!" Be honest with yourself, now!

If it just so happens you are a man reading this, then let's hope your response when you see this woman is to LOOK AWAY! LOOK AWAY! Unless, of course, she is your wife.

Back to you, LADIES. Now, upon being introduced to this woman, how might you treat her? What kind of "look" would you give her?

The saddest thing is that women who dress inappropriately do not always know they are attracting attention to themselves in such a way. Modest women sometimes assume that immodest women are purposefully out to steal their man. That could very well be true, however if you look into the hearts of these women, you discover that they have a deep hole they are trying to fill. They feel unloved and unattractive, and if they dress this way they get attention that makes them feel noticed. Often times, there is not a woman who wants to come alongside the woman and show her the way that pleases the Father. I hear women say it all the time, "they should know better!" And yet, they don't.

Romans 2:12-15 talks about those who do not know the Law, telling us that God does not judge them in the same way as He judges those of us who do know the Law. Those of us who do know the Law (the Bible) will be judged according to whether or not we ACT upon our knowledge.

It breaks my heart, because that girl could have been me. Had I not a dear friend who loved me and told me the truth in a loving way, I might have been cast out of the fold at a young age. I was so blessed to have wonderful women and men to tell me if I was dressing or acting inappropriately. Thank God they loved Him enough to tell me the truth in a gentle way, that made me want to change and drew me closer to Jesus rather than further from Him.

Romans 2:4 says that God's kindness is what leads us to repentance. Time and time again, I have experienced the kindness and goodness of the Lord. His compassionate love is unfailing, His mercies are new morning after morning!
Lamentations 2:22-23

Bravo! to those of us who can look past tattoos, cleavage, foul language, head coverings, gender confusion, whatever it may be, and embrace people as they are.

When He was here in the flesh, Jesus was known as a man who would look past the outside of a person and see the soul. He sees the part of us that will either live with Him in eternity or be separated from Him forever. He does not want to be separated from anyone. Let's follow His perfect example.

One of Mother Teresa's most memorable quotes comes to mind, "I see Jesus in every human being. I say to myself, this is hungry Jesus, I must feed him. This is sick Jesus. This one has leprosy or gangrene; I must wash him and tend to him. I serve because I love Jesus."

How do we stray so far away from what is taught in the gospels?   How many of the expectations we have on one another are based upon the religion of men, not upon that of God?

Whether we grew up in church or have never set foot in one, we need to ask ourselves if we might have faulty thinking about people and the way things should be. I think the world would look very different if we each stopped being mad at everybody for screwing up the planet and owned up to how much of the screw-up had to do with us.

On the other side of all of this, though, we who are reading our bibles and proclaiming the good news ought to remember that as quickly as we need to accept all people and embrace them where they are at, we also need to continue to walk purely with our God. We who know the teaching in the bible should know that the loving person should not cause the weaker believers to stumble. We set the example for them.

"It is good neither to eat flesh (meat), not to drink wine, nor anything whereby your brother is made to stumble, or is offended, or is made weak." Romans 14:21

Which Camp Will You Choose?

We always have a choice to make, don't we? Sometimes I forget that I can make a good choice.

Especially when it comes to picking veggies over sugar carbs. We also have a choice between two camps of "thought."

We can choose the rocky, barren terrain on the side of the mountain that faces the sun. This is the camp where we judge, condemn, and blame others.

Then there is the camp that sits in an enchanting meadow, with plenty of shade trees and a river close by (but not too close, so don't be thinking about mosquitoes!). This is the camp where we admit to ourselves that we are flawed, and seek to love people and believe the best of others.

I am guilty of setting up my tent in both of these camps. So ask yourself, which camp do you like better? Or perhaps a better question you can ask yourself might be: Which kind of person would you rather spend time with?

The message of Jesus was that we forgive one another—as He has forgiven us—and that we love others as we love ourselves. Yet it looks to me like this is the teaching of Jesus that we see lived out the least among churchgoers.

With that said I want to point out that there are some beautiful people I know who actually model this kind of Christianity, and those are the people who I want to hang out with the most because I want them to rub off on me!

I think overall, church people (I **am talking to myself here** *and possibly you too*) need to improve in the area of loving others to the point of forgiveness.

The Way of Love
1 Corinthians 13:5 "Love thinketh no evil..."
Ps. 15:3 "Nor taketh up a reproach against his neighbor"

> If all of us, by the grace of God, lived in the spirit of these two verses, think of the time that would be set free for prayer for those who do not know Him, if we had not to spend so much on those who do.
>
> It should be simply impossible for us to think unkindly of anyone. Satan will always see to it that there are people ready to sow seeds of suspicion. Let us refuse to receive them. Let us not imagine evil in our hearts, but always put the best and most loving construction on everything. Unkindness in our thought life is one of the things God hates.
>
> "Beloved, let us love..." (1 John 4:7)
> from Amy Carmichael's Whispers of His Power.

God's love is so much greater than our own capacity to love. We are proud and haughty by nature. Every one of us has things to which we say, "I would never do that," because the underlying idea is that we think to ourselves, "I am too good to do that." We are deceiving ourselves.

A Mirror of Truth

Proverbs 6:16-19 is a good mirror to look in. (16) "These six things doth the Lord hate; yea, seven that are an abomination unto Him: (17) A proud look, a lying tongue, and hands that shed innocent blood, (18) An heart that deviseth wicked imaginations, feet that be swift in running to mischief, (19) A false witness that speaketh lies, and he that soweth discord among brethren." (KJV)

When I think about the times I have been filled with pride, or I have judged another person (yes, I am guilty), it all started with me forgetting where I came from. If you have been walking with the Lord a while, it is important to remember who you were before Christ saved your sorry neck! Otherwise we can get all puffed up, thinking we are so pure and "holier than thou."

Why do we partake in communion? Is it not to remember what Christ has done for us? He has set us free. Without Him, none of us is able to love without conditions. We were once on a path that led to destruction. We have been redeemed! Now we have a new destination. We are heirs with Christ. We belong to Him. As His kids, we have access to all the love, joy and peace that flow from His eternal springs!

Lest You Trap Yourself

Warning! One of the most dangerous cages we can build for ourselves begins when we choose to hold a grudge against somebody. Any grudge will do just fine for building your little cage, whether miniscule or super-size.

We tend to forget that while we are harboring a grudge, we are actually building a cage that is keeping us "in." It feels like we are in control while we are building our cages. But before we become aware of it, we find ourselves trapped. Our offender(s) might even be free as a bird on the outside.

There is not freedom or joy in the cage. We are not able to allow the love of God into our heart inside the cage. The only way out of the cage is to forgive the offender. No matter what that person has done, in order to know God's forgiveness and the freedom He has to offer, we must first forgive others and let go of all grudges.

The offender may deserve punishment. They may deserve the death sentence. But unfortunately, my precious friend, we all deserve the death sentence. Until we come to the realization that we ourselves are undeserving of God's love, until we see our own wretchedness in light of God's pure goodness, we cannot fully know God's redeeming love.

LOVE conquers all. Even the "I Would Nevers."

We don't see the invisible realm at work around us, but it is real. When we choose to hold onto bitterness, we are giving Satan permission to mess with us.
When we choose to forgive as Christ forgives us, Satan no longer holds power over us. It is a real chain, invisible to our eyes, but nonetheless it is real in another dimension—the Kingdom of Heaven.

The power that comes from forgiveness is HUGE, people! HUGE! Likewise, the destruction from not forgiving is just as immense. Why else would Jesus tell us to: "pray for our enemies" (Matthew 5:44)?

2 Action Challenges

"For if ye forgive men their trespasses, your heavenly Father will also forgive you. But if ye forgive not men their trespasses, neither will your Father forgive your trespasses." Matthew 6:14-15   KJV

JOURNAL

Read 1 Corinthians 13

1. Each day, write down a few verses from 1 Cor. 13 in your journal. Ask God to replace your own human ability to love with His supernatural kind of love that is listed in the verse.

2. On the opposite page, write down the names of specific people who come to mind who you want to pray for. Perhaps people you have judged, or who have judged you in the past. Commit to pray for those people. Specifically pray for God to bless them, to forgive them, and to make Himself known to them.

One of my favorite authors and speakers, Debbie Alsdorf, often suggests to write out Bible verses on sticky notes and leave them all over your house, your bathroom mirror, refrigerator, etc. This is a great way to keep God's word on our minds and hearts.

3

Well, Shut My Mouth!

As a pastor's wife, I have seen people leave our church over the years for many different reasons. I do believe there are times we need to move on from one place of worship to another. However, when that happens we should be able to maintain healthy and good relationships with the people of the church we left. After all, the church is not just one little place of fellowship, it is wherever followers of Jesus congregate.

But too many times people leave in anger. They end up causing a lot of hurt and pain by their words or actions on their way out. Worse yet, because of social media, some people go so far as to post things on social media sites causing the church to be slandered in a more universal and serious way.

In turn, the church members who remain at the church take an offense and feel betrayed and hurt by the ones who left. The pastor and leaders are left behind to pick up the pieces of debris left by those who stormed off. I have found it to be the number one reason people stop going to church or decide they will never set foot in one. It is also one of the top five reasons pastors resign.

This experience has been teaching me that when someone hurts me or severs a relationship with me in anger, it is a huge opportunity to demonstrate God's love and forgiveness to them. It is also a way to foster healing to all the people who are aware of the situation. In fact, I am learning that the world can see the power of God's love in a greater way when we choose to bless those who curse us. Bless those who curse our loved ones. Bless those who,

When someone hurts me or severs a relationship with me in anger, it is a huge opportunity to demonstrate God's love and forgiveness

by their tongues, are bringing a negative reputation to Christ's body, His church. Most of the time people do not know how hurtful their actions are. Really, they don't. They are blind to their own actions. If we examine our own heart, can we truly say we are innocent in this area ourselves? We each have to guard the tongue, don't we?

Please don't think I am a guru or master at this just because I am writing it in a book. Do you realize that most people who write the books are simply imparting their own wisdom and experience? I am experienced at failing a whole lot! This ole girl here is a serious work in progress, with yellow tape all over the place!

No, I'm not claiming this to always be easy for me. There are prickly people in my life who I have a difficult time loving. You know, the kind of people who remind you of a porcupine?

At times I want to say, "God bless you," with a whole different meaning behind those three little words. But I have a choice whether to choose "stinkin' thinkin'" or to believe the best and follow in the footsteps of Jesus.

I've told you my own thoughts on this subject. But now let's read what the Authority has to say regarding this matter.

Booty-Kicking Jimmy

Good ole James. If you need to be set straight, you can count on the ole Jimmy to give you a good talking to. Here is what he has to say to us in James 3:1-12 KJV

"My brethren, be not many masters, knowing that we shall receive the greater condemnation.
2 For in many things we offend all. If any man offend not in word, the same is a perfect man, and able also to bridle the whole body.
3 Behold, we put bits in the horses' mouths, that they may obey us; and we turn about their whole body.
4 Behold also the ships, which though they be so great, and are driven of fierce winds, yet are they turned about with a very small helm, whithersoever the governor listeth.
5 Even so the tongue is a little member, and boasteth great things. Behold, how great a matter a little fire kindleth!

6 And the tongue is a fire, a world of iniquity: so is the tongue among our members, that it defileth the whole body, and setteth on fire the course of nature; and it is set on fire of hell.

7 For every kind of beasts, and of birds, and of serpents, and of things in the sea, is tamed, and hath been tamed of mankind:

8 But the tongue can no man tame; it is an unruly evil, full of deadly poison.   9 Therewith bless we God, even the Father; and therewith curse we men, which are made after the similitude of God.   10 Out of the same mouth proceedeth blessing and cursing. My brethren, these things ought not so to be.

11 Doth a fountain send forth at the same place sweet water and bitter

12 Can the fig tree, my brethren, bear olive berries? either a vine, figs? so can no fountain both yield salt water and fresh."

3 Action Challenge

The tongue is tricky to tame indeed. I bet every one of us would be found guilty, unless you are mute. Yes, we are all guilty if we examine ourselves honestly and carefully. So then, how do we grow from here? Or a more fitting question might be to ask, "How do we keep our mouths shut?"

1. Pray for God to transform your heart and mind. Pray for the power of Holy Spirit to be evident in your life.

"I can do all things through Christ Jesus who gives me strength" (Phil. 4:13).

As James points out, "Who can tame the tongue?" It is out of our control. But that is why we rely on the Spirit of Christ. When we decide to follow Jesus because we agree Jesus is God and Savior, when we invite Him to be our Lord and live in us, He gives us the ability to do all things through His strength.

Granted, we still mess up. But if we are talking to God throughout the day and bending our ear to hear Him, we become more aware of what He wants us to do and what he wants us to say and not say. Yes, He even gives us the ability to shut our mouths!

True, we will still blow it. But be encouraged that when we blow it, God often allows us to fail so that He can prove Himself in our weakness. In our weakness, He is strong. Also, be encouraged that as you continue to bend your ear to hear the Lord and as you make it a habit to ask Him to lead you in all things, He is faithful to do what you ask of Him. You will see victory in this area!

2. Pray and ask God to reveal to you if you have hurt someone by something you have said to them or about them. Write what is revealed in your journal.

3. Say you're sorry!   If you are aware of a time when you have spoken badly of someone to others, then the first thing you need to do is to go to that person and apologize.

 They may or may not forgive you, but you will have done your part in it. Often we may simply be repeating a rumor about someone or even some business, organization, or church. We forget there are people associated with every organization, and it is amazing how things tend to get back to people.

Take a quiz to see if you know what the Bible teaches us about gossip. (Answers are at the end of this chapter.)

1.) _____ revealeth secrets: but he that is of a faithful spirit concealeth the matter.
   a. A lying tongue
   b. An unbridled tongue
   c. talebearer
   d. A whisperer

2.) A false witness shall not be unpunished, and he that speaketh lies shall _____.
   a. be punished severely
   b. dwell carelessly
   c. perish
   d. stumble

3.) As coals are to burning coals, and wood to fire; so is _____ to kindle strife.
   a. a contentious man
   b. a contentious woman
   c. contention between neighbors
   d. a whisperer

4.) The words of a talebearer are as wounds, and they go down _____.
   a. into the innermost parts of the heart
   b. into the innermost parts of the belly
   c. from the top of the head to the sole of the foot
   d. into the uttermost parts of hell

5.) A lying tongue hateth those that are afflicted by it; and
_____ worketh ruin.
   a. the mouth of the wicked
   b. a deceitful mouth
   c. a lying mouth
   ✓d. a flattering mouth

6.) There is that speaketh like the piercings of a sword: but
the tongue of the wise is _____.
   ✓a. health
   b. slow to speak
   c. joy and peace
   d. as ointment poured forth

7.) An hypocrite with his mouth destroyeth his
neighbor: but through _____ shall the just be delivered.
   a. wisdom
   ✓b. knowledge
   c. judgment
   d. the intervention of the avenger

8.) _____ are in the power of the tongue: and they that love
it shall eat the fruit thereof.
   a. Sickness and health
   b. Goodness and evil
   c. Destruction and decay
   ✓d. Death and life

9.) Where no wood is, there the fire goeth out: so where there is no talebearer, _____.

    a. there is life and peace
    b. the brethren dwell in unity
    c. there is no contention
    d. the strife ceaseth

10.) The heart of the righteous studieth to answer: but the mouth of the wicked poureth out _____.

    a. slander
    b. foolishness
    c. evil things
    d. lies

11.) The lips of the righteous know _____: but the mouth of the wicked speaketh forwardness.

    a. what to say to the brethren at the gate
    b. what is acceptable
    c. what maketh peace
    d. what sootheth the troubled soul

12.) A prudent man concealeth knowledge: but the heart of fools proclaimeth _____.

    a. foolishness
    b. flattery
    c. ignorance
    d. madness

I recall the wise words of my Senior Pastor Steve Madsen, Cornerstone Fellowship Livermore, "If it isn't your own story, it isn't your story to tell." Sadly, most of the destruction in churches can be traced back to gossip. James tells the story well. The tongue is a vicious weapon.

I don't know about you, but I am thinking this chapter addresses one of my greatest challenges! Without the power of Jesus in me, I am sure to ram my head into a cement wall.

Nonetheless, I am willing to work on the following things:

- To strive to be a peacemaker.
- To strive to build bridges in relationships, rather than burn them down.
- To allow God to work in my life.
- To be slower to speak & slower to anger.
- To be a person who has a reputation of one who can be trusted with secrets.

When one of us blows it, (because we surely will!) let's choose forgiveness and understanding rather than take up a quick offense.

What do you say? Are you going to give it your best shot? Shall we spit on our palms now and shake hands?

1 Peter 3:8-12 *"Finally, be ye all of one mind, having compassion on one another, love as brethren, be pitiful, be courteous: Not rendering evil for evil... but contrariwise with blessing; knowing that ye are thereunto called, that ye shall inherit a blessing. For, he that would love life and see good days, let him refrain his tongue from evil and his lips that they speak no guile. Let him eschew evil and do good; let him seek peace and ensue it. For the eyes of the Lord are over the righteous and his ears are open unto their prayers, but the face of the Lord is against them that do evil."* KJV

Answer Key to Gossip Test:

1. talebearer Prov. 11:13
2. perish Prov. 19:9
3. a contentious man Prov. 26:21
4. innermost parts of the belly Prov. 26:22
5. a flattering mouth Prov. 26:28
6. health Prov. 12:18
7. knowledge Prov. 11:9
8. death and life Prov. 18:21
9. the strife ceaseth Prov. 26:20
10. evil things Prov. 15:28
11. what is acceptable Prov. 10:32
12. foolishness Prov. 12:23

Chaos Becomes Quiet

w/m by Kim Krenik

Life is broken, people are blistered
But You are near
Words can tear down, rip and divide us
You see You hear
You are near, closer than my beating heart
You don't run, when I yell and scream
I look, there you still are

Chorus:
You are nearer than my own breath
You Turn me like the tides
Turn me like the tides
I let go of every offense
And the noise finally subsides
Chaos becomes quiet
Chaos becomes quiet

I have shot out piercing arrows
With my own tongue
I've been wounded by my brothers
You're close enough
To redeem and heal infinite scars
To break through the walls of granite hearts

4
Thrown Off Every Chain

As you choose to shine your light outside of your own home and into your community, you may or may not be aware of this important fact: You become target practice for the enemy's minions. But I have a feeling they are not the cute yellow minions we all adore so much.

Yes, we follow Jesus. He is all-powerful. His children have nothing to fear. But we also have a real enemy. He doesn't care so much if you say you are a Christian. There's a whole lot of that going on. But if you act like a follower of Christ, then he gets grumpy. The last thing an enemy of Christ wants for you to do is actually reflect God's glory. He would rather have you bound up in chains. Those chains might look like a whole variety of different things. Maybe your greatest chain is a television show, or chugging beer by the barrels, or maybe it is a bad relationship or spending money you don't have on frivolous things.

I have plenty of my own chains that I am continually crying out to be freed from. As my life has become fuller with four kids and the hours in a day get gobbled up faster than they used to, I can easily neglect to write, to read God's word, to journal and reflect, and to write songs. I would rather chill out and watch a meaningless television show at night.

But I was convicted a few years ago that those hours I was spending during the week watching television could be used for His purposes. I decided to claim that time to work on my songwriting and to finish this book.

Another one of my terrible tendencies is to eat junk food when I am stressed out, and I am a poor meal planner, which leads to grabbing the worst kinds of food for my family because we are always on the run. I'm not getting any younger, and my body doesn't react well to processed foods anymore. I know the difference between clean eating and getting a binge beating. The effect of poor eating habits is low energy, depression, and lethargy, and it leads to unhealthy self-esteem. It also leads to diabetes and other horrible health issues. This is a real chain that the Lord is able to break. But I have to agree with him and do my part, don't I? Yep, I need prayer in this area! If you want to say a prayer for me right now while you are thinking about it, I will receive it!

The way we can identify a "chain": Does it keep you from the purpose God has for you? Is it an addiction? Does this activity or person keep you from spending time that you could be using to carry out a higher calling? The chain will be a time stealer, for sure. Often a chain will lead to shortening our physical lives!
How do we get freed from chains? First off, we cry out to the one who has the power to break every chain: Jesus!

Part of crying out to God is retreating to His Word. The Bible is our life treasure! Within this amazing book are answers you seek. God speaks to us in the Book of the Prophet Isaiah about breaking chains. Read Isaiah Chapter 58 - the entire chapter so you grasp the context of the passage. The point of this passage is not to command you to fast. It is to tell you why fasting should be done…to break every chain! When we fast from food for the

The chain will be a time stealer, for sure. Often a "chain" will lead to shortening our physical lives.

purpose of breaking a chain, it means we are serious. Think about the times your mind has been set on something, and you have given up food. It may have been a time you lost a loved one. It may have been after hearing heart-breaking news. That is the state of mind we choose to take on during a fast. The Purpose and Intent of your fasting is what God sees. If we fast because we want to look like "Super Jesus Freaks," but we are fighting with our spouse and kids, filled with anger and strife, God tells us in Isaiah 58 He does not hear our prayers. That's not good.

Is your heart broken over your marriage? Do you have habits you desperately want to change? God wants to set us free from our oppressor, Satan. He is a real enemy and our chains are real hindrances blocking us from the purpose God wants to carry out through each one of his children.

If we really want to have changed lives, we need to know Jesus and our actions will show we are His. How do we get to know Him? We need to start reading what He said and did. Study His life: Who did He hang out with? What did He teach in the parables? Everything you need to learn about Him is in the Bible. The letters in red in the four gospels, Matthew, Mark, Luke and John, were the words of Jesus when he was on the Earth. Both the Old and New Testaments are both filled with book after book and letter after letter that are all pointing to Jesus.

4 Action Challenge

Read John 15—Jesus' teaching on how to remain in Him.

JOURNAL

1. What are some practical ways we choose to "remain in Him" as Jesus commands in this passage? (Vs 10, 12, 13, 17)

2. If you follow Christ, who will hate you? (Verse 18)

3. Why does the world hate you? (Verses 19-25)

4. What hope do we have that we will be able to remain in Christ? (John 15:26)

5. Who is the Counselor and where does he come from? (Verse 26) What does he do? (John 16:7-15)

6. Ponder these things in your heart. Write down what you are discovering about Jesus as you read John 15.

7. Read the entire book of John and write down what you discover about Jesus as you ask the following questions:
   - What did He do?
   - What did He say?

- How does that affect you right now in your current situation and circumstance?

8. List one (or more) specific action you can take to live out what you are learning from this passage. Pray for the strength and mindset to carry out the action(s) you have written down.

You've Thrown Off Every Chain

w/m Kim Krenik

Verse 1:
Once I was lost, now I am found
Once I was blind, now I can see
I was in pieces, Now I am whole
I was in prison, now I am free

Chorus:
You've thrown off every chain (repeat)

Verse 2:
I was a slave to shame and regret
Wore dirty rags, you received me like that
You washed me clean, you gave me new clothes
You changed my name, I became yours

Chorus:
You've thrown off every chain (repeat)

Bridge:
You set my feet up on the mountaintop
You carried me through, carried me through every pain
You never gave up on me failures and all
When all the rest of the world walked away
You stayed by my side, you heard my cries
Lifted up high my weary, desperate soul
And now I am sure I'll always be yours
You'll keep me close, never let me go

5

Don't You Fret

One of the things I really don't enjoy about myself is that I worry about too many things. I worry about whether we will have a paycheck next month. I worry about my kids playing sports and getting hurt. I worry about whether our nation's security will be breached once again. I worry about our economy. God help me; I worry too much.

True, I don't watch the news much because it makes me worry more.

If you weren't feeling worried a minute ago, you probably are starting to feel it creep in now. Sorry....

But don't worry. I am here to encourage you with some ancient truth that comes down from springs that flow where water is eternal. When this water touches your lips, it has the power to remove your worry, anxiety, depression, and hopelessness. This is a water that will replace your fear with peace. It is a drink like no other drink that gives you not only your life, but abundant life.

You will find this wellspring of life in the Book of Psalms. Chapter 37 was written by David as an exhortation – not a complaint or a cry out to God, not a prayer, but a proclamation and a word for you and for me to ACT upon.

What is the first thing we read as we open to this chapter? The words: "Fret not..."

"Fret not thyself because of evildoers; neither be thou envious against the workers of iniquity." Psalm 37:1 *KJV*

Okay, so what were my worries I listed? I bet you have the same worries as I do; they are universal. Terrorists are something we tend to be a bit worried about these days. But what did we just read?

Don't worry about them. Don't envy them. "But wait a second," you might reply. "Why shouldn't I worry about the bad guys in the world?" Read on, pal.

Verse 2: "For they will soon fade like grass and wither like the green herb."

Hmmm. They will fade. That's true. Everything on this earth comes to an end, doesn't it?

We just had a shift of focus here. Did you see that? Did you see how one minute your eyes could only see the lateral view, but the next minute the lateral view blurred and suddenly the view became multi-dimensional?

Infinity and Beyond

Are you aware that there is another dimension that we don't usually pay attention to? There is a whole entire realm all around us that we can't see, unless we are looking for it.

In the New Testament, the letter to the Ephesians talks about the invisible realm.

Ephesians 6:10-12

"Finally, my brethren, be strong in the Lord and in his the power of his might. Put on the whole armour of God, that ye may be able to stand against the wiles of the devil. For we wrestle not against flesh and blood, but against principalities, against powers, against the rulers of the darkness of this world, against spiritual wickedness in high places."

When we start to see this other realm and look beyond our natural world, all the cares and worries of this world become dim. I am reminded of the beautifully crafted lyrics of the old hymn:

Turn your eyes upon Jesus
Look full in His wonderful face
And the things of earth will grow strangely dim
In the light of his glory and grace.

> dim: adjective of a light, color, or illuminated object; not clearly recalled or formulated in the mind.
>
> Verb
> to make or become less bright or distinct.

The Power of the Holy Spirit

Whenever you read scripture, did you know that you can ask the Holy Spirit to give you the ability to see beyond this dimension and into the invisible realm. Ephesians goes on to instruct us how we can stand up against our invisible enemies in Chapter 6:13-20. I broke this one down into two categories.

Pay attention to the ALLs in these next verses:

Action We Take	Reason for Action
Put on the whole armour of God	so when evil attacks you will be able to stand.
Stand firm in truth, Be ready to share good news Use your shield: FAITH	This puts out and deflects ll the flaming arrows of the evil one
PRAY on all occasions with all kinds of prayers and requests. ...stay awake with all perseverance praying for all Christ's followers	So that you are always ready To share your faith And to withstand the enemy And the battles in this life

There are some powerful things you can take away from Ephesians 6. I encourage you to spend time praying today. Allow God to seal these words on your heart and mind.

Philippians 4:4 tells us to :*"Rejoice in the Lord always; again, I say, "Rejoice!" Let your moderation be known to all men. The Lord is at hand."* KJV

That scripture addresses something important. Two things, actually. First it states to rejoice. Not one time, but twice! Why is it emphasized like this, do you think? Could it be that the author knows how difficult it is for us to rejoice? The people he addressed faced greater challenges than most of us face. They had plenty of reason to ask for a pity party. The same might be said for you right now.

The next thing I find important to take note of in this passage is the command to "Let your moderation.." (some translations say "gentleness") "be known to all."

What comes to your mind when you read that? Gandhi? The Horse Whisperer? In direct relation to worrying and fretting, think about gentleness. When you are worried, is your nature gentle? When we are relaxed we are gentle, but when we are anxious or stressed our physical movements are jerky and possibly even harsher, rougher than when we are calm.

Have you ever had a massage? Once the tension leaves your body, isn't your whole being more gentle and calm?

"The Lord is at Hand."

Philippians 4:5b goes on to say, "The Lord is at hand." That alone brings us a whole flood of emotions, doesn't it? Our Lord, the God who has already won every victory over sin and death, HE IS AT HAND! Other translations say, "The Lord is NEAR!" He is not far away, high above on his throne. He is near, close to you. Closer than you can imagine. Hallelujah! This should bring us comfort, peace, joy, elation, excitement, longing. I could go on...

Sometimes we can read over those four words, "the Lord is near" and miss the importance of them altogether. Music can be a powerful way to connect our hearts with our minds and help us to wholly grasp the things the Spirit wants to teach us.

I recently heard a worship song that helped me grasp those four words in a powerful way, bringing me to tears. I encourage you to listen to worship music to draw you to a deeper place of reflection.

Moving on in Philippians past that last powerful passage, it gets better. The words of Paul to the Philippians are an exhortation, a call to *action*, and a very awesome outcome:

Exhortation: "Do not be anxious about anything..."

Call to Action: "...in every situation, by prayer and petition, with thanksgiving, present your requests to God.

Very Awesome Outcome: "And the peace of God, which surpasses all understanding, will Guard your hearts and your minds in Christ Jesus."

Personal Guards

Do you realize you have access to your own personal *guard* in God's kingdom? The peace of God is listed here as a GUARD. We know Jesus is the Prince of Peace. We also know that if we confess with our mouths and believe in our hearts that Jesus is Lord, that He died for us all and was resurrected, the Holy Spirit (the Spirit of Christ, the Spirit of God) enters our hearts and makes himself at home inside us.

This is amazing news. It means we have access to everything God offers us. His *peace* is offered to us and will *guard* our hearts and our minds.

Fretting (read: Stress) brings about all kinds of evil. Medically, this includes heart attacks and all kinds of other health issues. But you are probably catching on to the fact that God doesn't want us to fret. Repeat the next challenges as often as needed (in addition to your annual massage). In my case, that's, ummm, Daily!

I pray you will find freedom from anxiety and worry as you act on what these verses instruct us to do.

Deep Breath In

w/m by Kim Krenik

You were like a diamond in a mine
Your sparkle was hidden in the dark
And now you are under the bright sun
Where you can shine, oh shine

Chorus
Let yourself laugh
Let the tears flow
Let yourself feel again
Hold nothing back
Let it all go
Throw all your worries to the wind
Take a deep breath in

All of those fears that pressed you in
Had you locked in a prison
They no longer have any power
You've broken free
Oh free   (Chorus)

Bridge
This is who you're meant to be. Radiant.
This is who you're meant to be
Shining and free

5 Action Challenges

Part 1: But Wait!
Read Psalm 37, the entire chapter because it is so very awesome!

Psalm 37 vs. 3 tells us to "Trust in the Lord, and do good;" Another meaning for the word trust here is "To wait for."

JOURNAL

1. Do you feel a bit restless sometimes? I can relate. Waiting is not my favorite. But what does the second half of this verse instruct?

2. ...and "do good" So what can we do while we wait? List some specific ways you can think of that would be Doing Good.

We can "do good." Well, at least that's something. There's nothing worse than waiting when you have nothing to do, is there? That is when the clock seems to tick along at half the speed.

The thing about waiting is that we tend to get ourselves into trouble sometimes while we wait, don't we? Perhaps you are waiting for that right person to come along, the love of your life, your soul mate.

I remember how hard it was at times to wait. Loneliness and longing can overtake us physically, mentally and emotionally. These are the times when we can be seriously compromised spiritually.

3. Think about the times in your past when you were waiting for something, and you got frustrated.
What did you do?   Did you do good?   Or not so good?

4. Do you have a desire you want God to fulfill? Write it down in your journal.

Think about what would happen if this desire were fulfilled. Will people think well of God if this desire is fulfilled? If so, it is more than likely a good desire.

The difficult thing to remember is that we still need to WAIT on the Lord to fulfill even His plans. Often his timing looks different from ours. There are many stories in the Bible about people who had to wait for the Lord to bring them out of difficult seasons and into times of blessing. Joseph, Jacob, Moses, and David are all inspirational examples.

5. Read Genesis 12:1-7   God promised to bless Abram and to make him a great nation (later his name gets changed to Abraham). How old was Abram at the time God made this promise according to verse 4?

6. Read Genesis Chapter 16. Abram had been faithful to his wife up to this point, and his wife still had no children. Do you think Abram and Sarai doubted God's promise at this point?

7. What do Abram and Sarai choose to do about the situation? (Verse 2)

8. What was the result of their choice? (Verses 4 -6)

     Even after experiencing the blessing of having four children, I still remember the pain caused during the six years when I was barren. I never lost hope or faith that God could do a miracle during that time, although there were times I came close. Others seemed to have lost hope for us though, and their lack of faith did try my emotions at times. Six years felt like a long time to wait. I am pretty sure after ten or fifteen years I probably would have given up hope.

I was 32 and Rob was 44 when we discovered we were going to have our first child. That seems like a late start to many people in today's culture. I can only imagine how Sarai and Abram must have felt, doubting that the child would come through Sarai in her old age.

9. Read Psalm 37: 3 - "Trust in the Lord and do good; dwell in the land and befriend faithfulness." (ESV) Would you say you are "befriending faithfulness" while you dwell in the land?

This is a difficult passage for me at times while I remain in the valley where I live. It can be dry, hot, monotonous, and downright difficult for me to want to do good or be faithful. I want to court a beautiful forest or a warm, sandy beach. I want to wake to the sounds of a bubbling creek and smell the scent of pines out my window. But day-in and day-out, I wake to the sound of cars on the busy street and the smell of cow manure.

However, I am reminded here in this passage to dwell in the land (that would be the land I am currently dwelling in, not the land I am dreaming about) and befriend faithfulness. I certainly need divine intervention for this, as it is one of the greatest challenges I face.

"Dwelling in the land" might mean your marriage, your church, your job, or your actual place of residence. Wherever we are, we are there for a reason, and we can squander away our days in misery, all the while missing out on amazing GOD appointments.

10. Read Psalm 37: 4 Does this bring you hope? It certainly does me! But don't forget verses 1-3 are the requirements. We must delight ourselves in Him, be faithful to Him, and wait for Him to act. Then He will give us the desires of our hearts.

11. Read Genesis Chapter 17. How old is Abram at this point?

12. How many years did Abram wait for God to fulfill his promise? (Remember he was 75 when the promise was first given.)

13. Read all of Psalm 37 again & steep in it.

This chapter is rich in truth and instruction for our daily lives! It encourages you to remember that the days on this earth go quickly. Think about that which is lasting and eternal!

Verse 16 "Better is the little that the righteous has than the abundance of many wicked. For the arms of the wicked shall be broken, but the Lord upholds the righteous." We could interpret that scripture literally today as "arms" = "weapons"!

Verse 23:   The steps of a man are established by the Lord, when He delights in his way; though he fall he shall not be cast headlong, for the Lord upholds his hand.

Soak in Psalm 37 awhile and let these scriptures permeate your mind. These words are a fountain of life. All who drink here will be satisfied!

Part 2: Fist Fights with Fret

Anxiety will creep in without our noticing it, even if we have found freedom from it one moment before. We may not attain heaven here on earth, but the Lord tells us to pray, "Your Will be done on earth as it is in heaven."

JOURNAL

Here are some more verses to memorize and help with fighting our foe we call FRET. (Not to be confused with Fred.)

1. Get those eyes back on Jesus. Read Isaiah 26:3 (Perfect peace!) and Matthew 14:22-33 (Peter walks on water when His eyes are on Jesus).

2. Choose to be thankful rather than wallow in self-pity and complaints. Read Phil. 4:4-7.

3. Take every thought captive. Read 2 Corinthians 10:3-6.

4. _Write down the things that you are becoming aware of as you read God's word and renew your mind.

In the Lord of the Rings trilogy, one of my favorite moments in the story is when the eagles swoop down and rescue the heroes. The reason this is so moving and powerful to me, is because it is a fitting illustration of one of my favorite passages in scripture. Isaiah 40:31 *"But they that wait upon the Lord shall renew their strength; they shall mount up with wings as eagles; they shall run and not be weary; and they shall walk, and not faint."* KJV

6
Burn, Baby, Burn

Have you ever been told that as you spend time with Jesus, you will start to look more like Him? I don't know whether I look anything like Him or not, but one thing I have discovered is that the more time I spend at the feet of my Savior, the more I become aware of the areas in my life that are keeping me from being closer to Him. He is absolute purity and whatever is impure can't be in His presence. That is why our daily time reading the Bible is so crucial and having a continual dialogue with God is so essential.

With that said, it is really important that we don't get puffed up when we are reading our Bibles daily and behaving ourselves. We are the funniest creatures, aren't we? One minute we sin and blow it; the next we get it right for a few weeks and do all the right things, and we are wagging fingers at our friends, husbands, and children, as if we are so high and mighty.

It is by the GRACE of God ALONE that we have any desire in us to do God's will and not our own. That is why the psalmist writes "Walk HUMBLY with our God."

Eph 2:1-10 KJV {1} And you [hath he quickened], who were dead in trespasses and sins; {2} Wherein in time past ye walked according to the course of this world, according to the prince of the power of the air, the spirit that now worketh in the children of disobedience: {3} Among whom also we all had our conversation in times past in the lusts of our flesh, fulfilling the desires of the flesh and of the mind; and were by nature the children of wrath, even as others.

{4} But God, who is rich in mercy, for his great love wherewith he loved us, {5} Even when we were dead in sins, hath quickened us together with Christ, (by grace ye are saved;) {6} And hath raised [us] up together, and made [us] sit together in heavenly [places] in Christ Jesus: {7} That in the ages to come he might shew the exceeding riches of his grace in [his] kindness toward us through Christ Jesus.

{8} For by grace are ye saved through faith; and that not of yourselves: [it is] the gift of God: {9} Not of works, lest any man should boast. {10} For we are his workmanship, created in Christ Jesus unto good works, which God hath before ordained that we should walk in them. –

Note: In this context, the Greek word for flesh (sarx) refers to the sinful state of human beings, often presented as a power in opposition to the Holy Spirit. There is an invisible world that hates the omnipotent God we follow. We have a real enemy.

Take special note of verse 8. And then 9. We will be tempted to boast when we get it right. I am sure pride is the sneakiest of all sins. Go back to this passage in Ephesians every day if you must and write it down. It is crucial that we remember that it is "by grace we have been saved—through faith. Not by works, that no man (or woman) may boast."

With that, we must also take action to get the "yuck" out of our lives so we can deepen our relationship with our precious Lover of Souls.

Have you heard that saying, "whatever dog we feed the most wins"? If we feed our minds with films, music, books, and friendships that oppose biblical truth, you can bet we are going to be influenced in the wrong direction. We are going to talk like and behave like the things we are putting into our minds. We all know that saying, what goes in, must come out.

There are things we need to stop doing and habits we need to break. I still have plenty of issues I need God to deal with in me, even after following Him for 30 years. In fact, I'm starting to realize that the longer we are on this planet, the more junk we collect. Metaphorically, as well as literally!

6 Action Challenges

Now, far be it from this author to tell the reader how to properly read this book! There are no instructions for use, simply use it in any way you see fit. It may be incredibly hot where you are; in that case, I am not offended if you should find that the book makes an excellent fan. (I admit I have had to do this myself.) I am glad it may be of use to you during a hot flash. If you don't care for it, at least give it away or leave it on a park bench or put it on someone's car windshield. Come on, be creative!

The only two things I pray you will not do is toss it in the trash or burn it. Except for the pages where I suggest you do so.

And so here we have come to the trashing and burning of pages.

There are some things that really do belong in the fire. Some disgusting qualities in ourselves that we absolutely abhor need to be tossed. Sometimes we may wait until the altar call at church to rid ourselves of these things rather than let these things go on a daily basis.

1. Right now, quiet your heart and take a minute away from your busy-ness.

2. Ask your Maker, "What is in me that You want to

bring out of me? Is there a root of anything disgusting to You that is keeping me from my total surrender? Anything keeping me from the joy that You have and the peace that You offer?"

3. And ... listen. Listen to Him because He is trying to tell you.

Once He reveals to you the "chains" He wants you rid of, open this book and write down what He reveals on these next couple pages. The "Burn Page". If you are new at listening to God, simply ask Him to reveal things, and then write down whatever comes into your mind.

<u>Burn, Baby, Burn!</u>

Pull out the burn pages and throw those tormenting "chains" into a fire. This could be as simple as a little metal can, or you may do what my friend Ali did with her husband and kids and have a family ritual in the backyard if you have a fire pit. (Or do it with your Bible study group in someone's fireplace.) Watch those things burn, baby. Burn into ash.

Burn, Baby, Burn!

Did you actually write down all the dark deeds and watch them burn up into smoke? I hope you did. And doesn't it feel so amazingly fine to be freed from all that messy "yuck" in your life?

Now replace the void left in your mind with something healthy for your mind, body, and spirit: God's impenetrable truth!

"Finally, brethren, whatsoever things are true, whatsoever things [are] honest, whatsoever things [are] just, whatsoever things [are] pure, whatsoever things [are] lovely, whatsoever things [are] of good report; if [there be] any virtue, and if [there be] any praise, think on these things." - Philippians 4:8 KJV

Whenever my kids want to know if they are allowed to play a certain video game or watch a certain film I remind them of this scripture. I often have to remind myself, as well!

Let's keep praying for each other in this area, as we are always faced with temptations to stray away from what is pure, good, and true. This is a challenge/exercise we should all be practicing on a daily basis. Well, except the burning thing might get a little out of hand.

7

Warrior Pose

Self-importance leads to impotence.
God-importance leads to omnipotence.

2 Chronicles 20 is a perfect illustration to us of what our worship should look like. It starts with a battle. Next, our recognition of the fact that we are helpless. Then our cry to God for help. Finally, our adoration of God.

Adoration, crying out to God, recognizing that He is the King of all kings, the One who has all dominion, who upholds us, who holds all things together in the palm of His hand. What a God we serve, what a concept that Christ dwells within us. Who am I that He calls me his own? To worship our God is to surrender all.

Being a singer, I have often read 2 Chronicles 20 and focused on the passage that says, "Put the singers in front," but this distracted me from the true intent of the passage. I was putting the emphasis on the singers. They got the glory, but the true focus here is not on the singers at all. God could have said, "put the children first," or "put the architects first", or "the masons." It wouldn't have mattered. It is the part that says,

"You will not even need to fight. Take your positions; then stand still and watch the Lord's victory. He is with you, do not be afraid or discouraged. Go out there tomorrow for the Lord is with you."

The focus is not on the singers and what they are doing here. The focus is on the Lord. He is the central focal point. The singers just have to stand still.

The other part of this passage that is worth taking note of: the singers sang praises to their God. They weren't singing to draw attention to themselves. They drew everyone's attention to their God's greatness.

God's power and voice were so overwhelming, her blunder was invisible to them in comparison to His presence.

My friend, Heather, read this chapter and shared her own example of a time when God's power worked through her, and all she had to do was be present, the vessel. I got her permission to share her story with you.

Heather was leading her women in a worship song, and in the middle of the bridge of the song she lost her sense of where things were around her as she was closing her eyes while playing the keyboard and singing. She banged her mouth into the microphone!
The surprise of hitting the microphone caused her to let out a loud cry in the middle of the song. She felt like she had totally muffed up the song at that point. Clearly most people would agree she blew that performance.

However, at the end of the song, several people approached her crying. They told her that God was speaking directly to them through the song. No one seemed to even notice her huge and obvious mistake. God's power and voice were so overwhelming that her blunder was invisible to them in comparison to His presence.

Joshua and the battle at Jericho give us another powerful example of how God works through humans to carry out His plans and how the strength of men has no comparison with the might of Jehovah. In Joshua 5, an angel of the Lord visits Joshua. With sword drawn, he tells Joshua he is the commander of the Lord's army. He tells Joshua to worship the Lord, for he is standing on holy ground. Then in Joshua 6 God uses his commander to give Josh a message. God says they will not have to fight because God is going to give the city of Jericho over to them. The only weapon to be used: the voice.

God calls Joshua and his army to sing and shout praises to God! You can read what happened next in Joshua 6.

Stand Still

Back in 2 Chronicles 20, the Israelites were commanded to "stand still." Whenever I have heard that expression, I have believed it to mean, stop and do nothing, but wait for God to show up. But there is a part of the message I was missing.

"All things are lawful for me, but all things are not expedient: all things are lawful for me, but all things edify not."
1 Cor. 10:23 KJV

As a soldier in battle, you have the enemy running at you. The arrows are flying, and they are aimed at your chest. We are talking battle here. Think about it: Would you be able to stand still and not run for your life is a bunch of huge men with swords were coming toward you, intending to kill you?   I have dreamed this was happening to me. Believe me, I wanted to run.
It is not so easy to stand still, now is it? What would you tend to do? Run? Hide? Fight back? This passage is talking about an army in the midst of an attack. How does this apply to us today?

We are in an invisible battle. We have a real enemy who is storming our gates. We might have already been hit and knocked down. We might have our face in the dirt, and we might be feeling like we should just end it now before it can get any worse.

Get Up. Stand still. Take action. The action is to plant our feet in the ground and stand firm, with our shields locked. That is an action. It is not laying down and sleeping. Think of the mighty Spartans in 300AD. Those men were pure muscle and they stood with their feet planted and shields locked, an impenetrable force to be reckoned with.

Faith, without muscle, is dead.

Believe in the Lord your God and you will Be Able to stand firm and

- Not faint.
- Not give up.
- Not run away.
- Not hide and sleep.
- Not bury yourself in drugs, alcohol, an affair
- Not cave to impulsive spending or eating.
- Not ignore your problems by reading a novel, playing video games or watching a movie. (Me: totally guilty of this last one)

LEGALIST ALERT! Do not misunderstand me! Some of the things I just wrote in that list are not sins in and of themselves. Many of those actions in and of themselves are not wrong, on occasion or in certain circumstances. For instance, we have to run away sometimes from bad people or temptation. We have to sleep. We have to eat and there are things we will need to buy. Certain drugs might be needed for an illness. Movies, games and books are a nice way to chill out occasionally. Even an occasional glass of wine can be healthy for someone who is NOT an alcoholic. *Those things are not bad or wrong in or of themselves.*

Ya, I would hate you to become an army of legalistic, Nazi-like "Bible-thumpers" after reading this chapter. The takeaway here is to recognize that there is danger in thinking those things are the problem.

Those things are added blessings to life. 1 Corinthians 10:23 reminds us, "'I have the right to do anything,' you say—but not everything is beneficial. 'I have the right to do anything'—but not everything is constructive." (NIV)

I don't know about you, but I have found that my tendency is to run to temporary fixes before running to my Savior. Unfortunately, those things will not be able to rescue me. They make a nice band-aid. But none of those actions count as "standing firm". Those are the natural reactions we have when faced with an enemy, but do not lead us to victory!

On the contrary, those things can make us the enemy's captives. When we choose to not stand firm, we instead surrender ourselves to the enemy to do what he wants with us. And you can bet your life on this: He wants nothing more than to take us away from our Mighty Warrior God who is our Defender.

Stand Firm and Sing God's Praise

Are you facing cancer or a disease? Do you have fear that has you bound to a post where you are afraid to leave? Start singing. Praise your God and proclaim His greatness.

Open your Bible and read the words and sing, even shout them out. You don't have to have a pretty voice to do this.

The next part is to watch the Lord's victory. What an awesome privilege, to be on the side of the conqueror and great victor! The Bible tells us that JOY will be our strength. Rejoice in trouble. Rejoice in being persecuted. God's ways are not our ways, are they?

Gratitude should always be in our arsenal of weapons!
Stay in the FIGHT!

Do not give up!

7 Action Challenges

1. Write down the following three scriptures on sticky notes and post them around your house. Each morning SAY them out loud. Better yet, SHOUT THEM! SING THEM! Remember, often times we need to ACT first to train our bodies to follow. This is a great way to fend off depression.

"And of thy mercy cut off mine enemies, and destroy all them that afflict my soul: for I [am] thy servant". Psalms 143:12 KJV

"Being confident of this very thing, that he which hath begun a good work in you will perform [it] until the day of Jesus Christ:" Philippians 1:6 KJV

"And we know that all things work together for good to them that love God, to them who are the called according to [his] purpose." Rom 8:28 KJV

2. Program your radio station or Pandora to a station that plays your favorite songs that have lyrics which speak about God and Who He is.

3. This week read 2 Chronicles 20—the entire chapter.

4. Write down the things you are thankful for each day in your journal. Thank God for each thing.

When you meet (or call) your friend or Bible study group, spend time thanking God together for all the things you have each written down. Sing songs together. If any of your group members wrote a song or a poem that week, ask them to share it. One or more of your group members may be gifted singers or musicians. Encourage them to lead the rest of the group in songs.

Warrior Pose

w/m by Kim Krenik

When darkness closes in
Fear has overcome
The air is so thick it could be cut
I can't breathe, I want to run
But don't want to lose ground

Come and be my arrow
Come and be my bow
I wait in the valley Of dark shadows
I will not be moved
I will not be thrown
I stand still waiting
In a warrior pose oh oh oh oh oh
Warrior Pose oh oh oh oh

My feet slip, I fall
Too tired to even crawl
No strength left to sing another song
Then I hear a trumpet sound
And I watch as my enemies fall down

Stand your ground, never Faint
Be strong, be brave, do not be afraid
Morning is breaking and darkness is overtaken

8
You believe... What?

If someone asks you what you believe and why you believe it, are you prepared to give an answer? Do you know what you really believe? Do you know who the people that wrote the Bible are? When they lived, who they hung out with, and who they were originally writing to?

The word "Christian" means "little Christ." It was actually a derogatory name the first century believers were called by the non-believing world. It referred to them as people who followed Christ, and at that time they were punished for doing so. Jesus Christ was considered to be an enemy to the ruler of Rome. Caesar was believed to be the king of all kings; the Roman Empire was the greatest nation in that time. Jesus was a threat to his power and authority over the people, and his followers suffered death as punishment.

We live in an age where people are able to get all kinds of information on the internet. Write down the questions you have and do some research to discover the answers. The best place to start?

The Bible, which has been written down, recorded, and preserved for you and for me to learn about our faith and where it all began. It is always best to start a story from the beginning, don't you think? Where is the beginning of your faith story?

Of course, our faith begins with our own personal experiences. How did Jesus change your life? This is called your "testimony." Your testimony is extremely powerful and useful to encourage others. You need to share your story!

But there is more than just your story that needs to be shared. If all we have is one experience to share, but we have no idea how to explain who Jesus is, what His character is, why He came, and why we follow Him, then our testimony doesn't have anything to really back it up, other than our own word. We need to go to a higher authority than just ourselves. So where do we go?

As followers of Jesus, our Authority is the Bible. The Book of Genesis is where it all starts. If your Bible study has thus far been like playing a game of Russian Roulette (in other words, flipping pages and reading a random scripture somewhere and then trying to decipher its meaning), then you need a little crash course in how to read a book, my friend! Would you pick up any other book, like say, a mystery, and flip pages, and then read it expecting to know what exactly was happening in the story? I hope not. I hope you would read from start to finish.

The account in Genesis of creation is one of those often-debated things in the Bible that a whole lot of people have thrown out as being impossible.

If this is a stumbling idea for you, then you have to ask yourself whether you can believe any of what a follower of Christ believes.

Do you believe Jesus was born of a virgin? Do you believe Jesus performed all the miracles written in the New Testament?

If not, then do you believe the Big Bang Theory is really possible? Do you believe all of creation came to be, all the order and perfect chemistry, every living thing all came into existence suddenly because of this massive collision of gasses in space? Do you maintain the idea that this planet and its perfect environment in which a human can exist just came to be out of nothing, without any intelligent designer behind it?

In case you haven't heard, Einstein came to the decision that there had to be an intelligent designer behind it all. At one time, so did Stephen Hawking. Of course, he has been known to change his mind...a few times. It never ceases to amaze me how so-called "brilliant" people put their trust in mortal men like Hawking and Einstein. Men who are here today and gone tomorrow.

You need to make a decision whether you believe it all or not. If you can't agree with the scriptures, you will not be able to live by the scriptures. Once you come to a place of agreement with the scriptures, only then can you be transformed by them.

Rev. 3:16 says "...you are neither hot, nor cold. But since you are lukewarm I will spit you out of my mouth." I read that as, "Make up your mind already."

Faith is a Gift from God

Are you aware that faith is something God gives to us? We don't have to conjure it up on our own. If you WANT to believe, but you struggle with doubt, say a prayer with that little mustard seed of faith inside you and ask God to break through your doubt. He has done it before for the most skeptical of us. He can increase your faith, too, if you ask Him.

If you are looking at the creation story through God's lens versus man's, you are going to see the verses in Genesis come into a whole new light.

When we search the scriptures, what is our purpose? Is it to know God? To feel His love? To know what He wants for us? From us? To know our purpose on this earth? To find hope, peace, and joy?

8 Action Challenges

Genesis Chapter 1:1-2:3   The Story of Creation

Read the book of Genesis.
1. Write down the questions you are asking in your journal.
2. Write down what it is you want as you read the Bible.
3. Write down the doubts you have.

NOTE: Remember to think of the things you want in terms of the spiritual and intangible rather than physical desires (i.e. we want joy vs. a new car or true peace vs. a massage!).

Yes, we can ask God for those things as well, and believe me, I am always asking! But our God who created us and knows us better than we know ourselves is able to heal us at the ROOT of whatever our issue is, not just cover us up with a temporary bandage.

The Wise King

2 Chronicles 1:7-12 KJV - *"In that night did God appear unto Solomon, and said unto him, Ask what I shall give thee. And Solomon said unto God, Thou hast showed great mercy unto David my father, and hast made me to*

reign in his stead. Now, O LORD God, let thy promise unto David my father be established: for thou hast made me king over a people like the dust of the earth in multitude.

Give me now wisdom and knowledge, that I may go out and come in before this people: for who can judge this thy people, [that is so] great? And God said to Solomon, Because this was in thine heart, and thou hast not asked riches, wealth, or honour, nor the life of thine enemies, neither yet hast asked long life; but hast asked wisdom and knowledge for thyself, that thou mayest judge my people, over whom I have made thee king: Wisdom and knowledge [is] granted unto thee; and I will give thee riches, and wealth, and honour, such as none of the kings have had that [have been] before thee, neither shall there any after thee have the like."

Our desire for material things of this world often kills our desire to know God.

God is concerned with your soul. Yes, He might bless us with material things at times, but if that is all you long for, then your desires are for temporal things that have no worth. They will burn up. You can't take them into eternity.

5. When God said, "It is not good for man to be alone," and then He made a helper for the man, what does that tell you about God?

6. When the scriptures tell us that God rested, what does that tell us about God?

9

Padded Knees

Intercessory prayer. The Calling of Every Believer.

I believe we are all called to pray and intercede for one another, for our national and statewide leaders and politicians, for our pastors and churches, and for our orphans and widows. The Bible is very clear on the purpose of prayer and on who is to pray.

The idea that prayer is only for those who have a gift to pray is something that is misunderstood and gets used as a cop-out. It is true that being able to pray is a God-given gift, but it is also true that once you decide to follow Jesus, you are automatically given the gift!

As soon as we become a follower of Christ, we have direct access to our Heavenly Father through His Son. We are privileged to "get" to talk to God. We have become His heirs.

Galatians 3:29 KJV - "And if ye [be] Christ's, then are ye Abraham's seed, and heirs according to the promise."

Galatians 4:4-7 KJV - "But when the fulness of the time was come, God sent forth his Son, made of a woman, made under the law,

To redeem them that were under the law, that we might receive the adoption of sons. And because ye are sons, God hath sent forth the Spirit of his Son into your hearts, crying, Abba, Father. Wherefore thou art no more a servant, but a son; and if a son, then an heir of God through Christ."

There you go; we all share the same amazing Dad. Pretty awesome, I say!

Is God Hearing Me?

Most people I know have admitted they sometimes feel like God isn't listening to their prayers. They could be right. According to the bible, there are a few things that can hinder our prayers:

1. When we don't forgive others:
Jesus said that we need to forgive others if we want our Father in heaven to forgive us.

2. Disbelief (doubt) hinders our prayers:
Jesus Himself is the intercessor between us and God. Jesus bridges the gap between us and God, so we now have access to God.

When we intercede for others, we have a few responsibilities. We need to ask him Jesus to cleanse our hearts from sin, to release forgiveness over our offenders, and to expect God is going to act (faith). We can ask the Father to heal others, even those who don't know God. We can pray and ask God to show mercy and to redeem another person.   God delights in us when we intercede. Jesus is our model for intercessory prayer. Jesus told his disciples that Satan longs to destroy each of them, but that he would intercede for them.

Samuel says in 1 Samuel 12:23, "Moreover as for me, God forbid that I should sin against the LORD in ceasing to pray for you: but I will teach you the good and the right way:"   If you are a Christian and you can't remember the last time you prayed on behalf of another, that is a good sign that you need to quiet your heart and have some one on one time with your Maker. The beautiful thing about our amazing God is that He is always ready to meet with us, even when we have ignored Him for years. The minute we return to Him, His arms are open wide, ready to welcome us home. I should know.
I have been the prodigal in my prayer life. One of the many wonders of God is that His mercies are new every morning and His compassions never fail us.

Sometimes we fail to pray because we feel like we don't know how. When Jesus walked the earth, His followers asked Him to teach them how to pray. In Luke 11 Jesus teaches about prayer. We can also learn from Jesus' own prayer times in John 17, where Jesus prays for Himself, His disciples, and all believers just before He was arrested and would no longer be with them.

Take the time to read these chapters in Luke and John over the next week. Carefully study them and apply them to your own prayer life. This would be a great step to take to grow closer to God and understand His purpose for your life.

Mysteries of Fasting

I am not an expert, but I can tell you a couple practical things I have discovered about fasting from my own experience: Fasting from food while praying brings clarity to our minds, which is the opposite of the natural effect of <u>not</u> eating.

Naturally, we need to maintain our blood sugar and not skip meals or we can get light headed and dizzy. Supernaturally, when we fast and are setting our mind on hearing God during a fast, we are able to hear Him more clearly. He may even open the floodgates of heaven to us. Answers to prayers come quicker. The spirit realm is a mystery to us, but something happens in God's dimension when we fast to seek God.

Fasting from food should cause us to feel weaker. However, when we fast in order to seek God for answers, He gives us a supernatural strength that can only come from His power and authority.

Fasting denies our flesh of something it craves. We are all made up of intellect, flesh, heart, and spirit. In denying our flesh, we are strengthening the spirit. This has to do with the "unseen," and it takes faith to understand this principle.

"Work as if you will live a hundred years, pray as if you will die tomorrow."
-Benjamin Franklin

I am not about to write a book on fasting because I really have limited experience. But I will tell you that in my personal experience, every time I fast, I see God send His answers quickly. I know Jesus himself modeled fasting for us. Therefore, it is important that we do it. As we practice what Jesus taught, we find that He will blow our minds with the things He shows us.

When I seek the Lord for direction, when I am desperate for some answers, I will usually fast. In the past, fasting has brought an answer quickly to me.

However, it isn't a magic formula. There is no guarantee it will bring an answer quickly every time. God is on the Throne. I can't tell the King of kings what He should do. When we pray we say to our Heavenly Father,

"Thy will be done," not "MY will be done."

I do expect God to act. It may not be in the way I ask Him to act, but He will act according to His will.

Make no mistake, I am not some "super-Christian" because I fast. In fact, I would rather not shout out about it because I know God doesn't like us to parade our prayers, and He doesn't want us telling others we are fasting. (Scripture references to this are in the Challenge ahead.)

It is so important that we don't think we are strong and amazing people because we fast and pray. No, we are still wretched and desperate. In fact we need to fast because we are desperate! We need a Savior. We should pray and fast because we need Him and want more of Him. We should pray and fast because we want others to know him and to be saved from the enemy of our souls.

Beware of becoming like a Pharisee, who wrongly believed themselves to be better than people who did not do fast. Come on, if you are truly so godly, don't you want others to be strengthened in their faith? Instead, pray that God will strengthen *all* His people. If you are praying and fasting and truly close to your God, your heart will be soft towards everyone, not judgmental. The result of spending time in God's presence is an increase of love in our hearts for others. God opposes the proud and lifts up the humble.

Did you know? Our founding fathers of this country fasted and prayed on many occasions, and the constitution's final draft is credited to the fact that only due to prayer and fasting could the men agree upon it. If this is interesting to you, read here different accounts in America's history when our founding fathers prayed and fasted:

February of 1775 the following proclamation was made: "For A Day of Fasting and Prayer" by the Honorable Jonathan Trumbull:
Esquire, Governor of the English Colony of Connecticut, in New-England in America; To offer up fervent Supplication to GOD, for His gracious Presence with us---to give us true Repentance and Reformation and to make us fully sensible that our Dependence must be on His Power and Grace alone, to deliver us from all the Evil we feel or fear;---that He would not leave us to trust in an Arm of Flesh

From The Proclamation, July 13, 1775, by Jonathan Trumbull, Lebanon, Connecticut, to George Washington:

The Honorable Congress have proclaimed a Fast to be observed by the inhabitants of all the English Colonies on this continent, to stand before the Lord in one day, with public humiliation, fasting, and prayer, to deplore our

many sins, to offer up our joint supplications to God,
for forgiveness, and for his merciful interposition for us in
this day of unnatural darkness and distress. They have, with
one united voice, appointed you to the high station you
possess.

What happened as a result of this proclamation?
A quote from David Ramsey's history states:

"Since the fast of the Ninevites, recorded in sacred writ,
perhaps there has not been one, which was more generally
kept, with suitable dispositions, than that of July 20th,
1775. It was no formal service. The whole body of the
people felt the importance, the weight and the danger of
the unequal contest, in which they were about to engage;
that every thing dear to them was at stake; and that a
divine blessing only could carry them through it
successfully.

This blessing they implored with their whole souls, poured
forth in ardent supplications, issuing from hearts deeply
penetrated with a sense of their unworthiness, their
dependence and danger; and at the same time, impressed
with an humble confidence, in the mercies and goodness of
that Being, who had planted and preserved them, hitherto,
amid many dangers, in the wilderness of a new world."

Prayer Requests

Prayer Request	Date of Request	Date of Answer

9 Action Challenges

1. Write down your requests to God and record every answer you get. Or if you are a journal freak like me, designate a separate journal as your Prayer Journal.

2. READ Jesus' teachings on prayer in Luke 11 & John 17. Take time daily this week to reflect on those two chapters and write down the things that are revealed to you.

3. The book of Matthew has a whole lot of things to teach us about prayer as well. Who does Jesus say we should pray for in Matthew 5:44? WHY should we do this? (According to Matthew 5:45-48)

4. Read Jesus' teaching in Matthew 6:5-18.
What reward does a hypocrite have to look forward to (Verse 5b)?

5. List some things Jesus instructs us NOT to do when we pray
Verse 5-6
Verse 7-8
Verse 15:
Verse 16:

6. What are some things Jesus instructs us To Do when we pray? List them and write down the reason the verse gives for these instructions:
Matthew 6:6
Matthew 6:9-13
Matthew 6:14
Matthew 6:17

7. Pray for our sons and daughters and cry out for the next generation.

Prayer Prompts
Need some prompts to help you pray? Here is a place to start:

1 Timothy 2:1-4:
"I exhort therefore, that, first of all, supplications, prayers, intercessions, [and] giving of thanks, be made for all men; For kings, and [for] all that are in authority; that we may lead a quiet and peaceable life in all godliness and honesty. For this [is] good and acceptable in the sight of God our Saviour; Who will have all men to be saved, and to come unto the knowledge of the truth."

Paul (who wrote the letters to Timothy) spells it out clearly for us, doesn't he?

Daniel teaches a lot about the importance of our prayers for our nation's leadership. Daniel 2:21. We often forget they have a direct impact on our way of life and our freedoms. We also forget that the God we serve is also the King above all other kings.

Our nation's leaders, lawmakers, law enforcers
Our state and city leaders in government.

In addition to the above, I have specified a few more prayer prompts:

- o Single adults who long to be married
- For strength, protection as they wait, patience to wait for the person God has for them, for wisdom to recognize whom they should or should not marry.
    - o Christian marriages to be strong and vibrant and to bring God glory.
    - o Healing for those who have been hurt by their spouses.
    - o Pastors and Christian leaders who are teaching and sharing God's word.
- For God to be their shield and strong tower and to protect them from the temptation they face to water down the teaching of God's Word, for protection from temptation in all areas, for peace in their homes and marriages.

- o If you are married or waiting to be: Pray for your spouse (or future spouse).
- That they will grow closer to Jesus, that they will experience God's love more intensely than ever before, that they will be protected from temptation.
  - o Pray for your children to learn God's ways and walk in His light and His love.
  - o Pray for the other children in your children's schools and in church.
  - o Pray for Christian teachers who teach our children to have a boldness and fresh filling of the Holy Spirit.
  - o For kids in public school, their teachers, principals, administrators, and office staff.

"To pray is our greatest privilege and our greatest calling." -Kay Smith, <u>The Privilege</u>

I encourage those of you who have your kids in public schools to pray every morning with your kids before they begin their school day. I believe praying out loud each morning with your children is a way to teach them that the most important thing we can do as we start our day is to talk to the Lord and put our trust in Him.

Don't beat yourself up if you have never done this with your kids! It is not ever too late to start doing these things if you haven't started yet, or to get back on track if it is something you have done in the past but have stopped. We do not live under condemnation. I am guilty of getting caught up in the whirlwind of busy-ness and neglecting my Bible reading times with the kids.

Forget what is behind and keep striving forward. Seize the day!

I have an amazing set of parents. But they were not churchgoers. At home, I wasn't taught the value of reading my Bible or praying. As a mom who is a churchgoer and a Bible reader, I make mistakes every day that I wish I could take back. I have to confess my sins daily, receive God's glorious forgiveness, and rely on His Holy Spirit to fill me and lead me down His path. I need God to teach me every how to be a better mom to my kids, a mom who directs her kids to have a closer relationship with Jesus. I have to remind myself that in my weakness, He is strong!

The same goes for you as well. God loves you. If you have kids, rest assured that He loves them far more than you do. You will not make the perfect choices every day as a parent, but You can trust Him to protect you and your children despite your mistakes.

Leaning Into You

By Kim Krenik

I'm leaning into You Before the branch breaks off
I've done all that I can And now I'm leaning
I feel the gusting wind Trying to throw me off
Pressing at my resolve And now I'm leaning

CHORUS
I can't hold on anymore
I can't stand against the storm
Need some divine intervention
So I'm leaning your direction
Leaning Into You

This twig that used to snap Is learning how to bend
Oh , learning how to trust again CHORUS

Bridge
Like a shelter on a mountain's edge
When the rains pour down, I run into it
I'm leaning into you
Like a cradle out in the raging sea
When the waves try to devour me
I'm leaning into you
When lightning strikes and I feel alone
I have a place to hide, I know just where to run
I'm leaning into you
When the thunder roars and I'm in the dark
You're the calming song, you're the burning spark

10 Faith Muscles

Romans 8 is one of my favorite chapters in the bible. To summarize it, this passage teaches us that once we choose to follow after Christ, we are free. We are no longer dead in our sin. Instead, we are very much alive. We are no longer slaves to fear. Instead we have overcome fear because Christ's Spirit (the Holy Spirit) dwells inside us.

Even more amazing is the part that tells us we are God's kids! We are His heirs, and that means whatever belongs to our heavenly Father also belongs to us! We can call to Him anytime because He is our caring and loving Dad. If you sit with that for a while, I am pretty sure you could blow your mind out thinking about the possibilities. In fact, as I am sitting now and thinking about it, God is comforting me once again with this passage. I needed to reflect on this today.

Read Romans 8 right now before you continue reading the rest of this chapter.

"[There is] therefore now no condemnation to them which are in Christ Jesus, who walk not after the flesh, but after the Spirit." -Rom 8:1 KJV

If you don't grasp the power and importance of this, I pray your eyes, ears, and heart will be opened by the Holy Spirit. This is tremendously good news! On the day Jesus died on the cross, a sinner's death, scorned as nothing more than a criminal of His day, the sins of the entire world were thrust upon Him. One man. One God.

Today, it is not easy to find people who embrace this truth. People believe all sorts of ideas and philosophies. People package their philosophies up nicely and put them into our children's textbooks, publish articles about their ideas, and make great claims that they have the proof for what they believe.

The truth is, they don't have the proof any more than I do. He took on the sins of the world. He rose from the dead. I believe it! I embrace the Good News. Every other religion, philosophy, and idea that I have explored I have found to crumble beneath Jesus.

Romans 8 starts with an explanation by the Apostle Paul regarding the power of what Jesus did on the cross. In this chapter, Paul explains a little about the Holy Spirit and how He works in us. I would simply say, when Jesus rose from the grave and took His place at the Right Hand of the Throne of God, He sent His spirit to fill those of us who choose to follow Him. His spirit is His person, residing inside of us.

Romans 8:12-17 tells us how to live and how NOT to live. This is an important reminder that we can all use a daily dose of. I don't know about you, but I am so easily sidetracked! This is why I need to read God's words in the Bible. My mind is like an alarm clock that has to be reset every day! One of my favorite parts of this passage starts in verse 14:

"For as many as are led by the Spirit of God, they are the sons of God. For ye have not received the spirit of bondage again to fear; but ye have received the Spirit of adoption, whereby we cry, Abba, Father. The Spirit itself beareth witness with our spirit, that we are the children of God: And if children, then heirs; heirs of God, and joint-heirs with Christ; if so be that we suffer with [him], that we may be also glorified together."   -Rom 8:14-17 KJV

Paul goes on to remind us that we have a future home. This earth, where we presently reside, will pass away. All creation knows this. The trees know they are dying, and they await the new earth when they will truly LIVE in the way God originally created them to live. I can't imagine how colorful the new earth will be. What we see here and now is only a shadow of what is to be seen in our future home.

Paul also encourages us in Romans 8:28-39 that we are more than conquerors!   Nothing can separate us from the love of God.
"…Neither death nor life, neither angels nor demons, neither the present nor the future, nor any powers, neither height nor depth, nor anything else in all creation, will be able to separate us from the love of God that is in Christ Jesus our Lord."

Slaves to Fear—Unshackled!

Romans 8 has too many amazing takeaways to settle on just one. But right now, take a minute to write down all the ways you have been a slave to fear. Remember, fear and worry are one and the same. I will help by giving you an example with my own list:

- Worried about what I will say in front of an audience
- Worried about our enemies in other countries
- Worried about a crisis, like an earthquake
- Worried about my kids

- Worried about an upcoming test
- Worried about people at church looking down on me for missing a church event
- Worried about my house being messy and someone gossiping about it
- Worried about a big red pimple that appears on the day we scheduled for a Christmas card photo shoot

The list could go on, but I can already see eyes rolling and in some cases, heads rolling. Yikes…You might want to strangle me and burn the entire book if I did that to you!

Now it is your turn. Write down your list of fears. You have done this before, but chances are you still have fear to contend with. So come out with it!

Now read Romans 8:26-39 as many times as it takes for you to let it morph your thoughts from Fearful to Faithful. Write it down on sticky notes and note cards. Leave them all over your house. Soak it in, baby. Let it steep like tea leaves in a china teapot until you have it flowing strongly through your veins!

Steps of Faith

When I turned twenty years old, three friends and I decided to start a worship band. We were at one band member's house rehearsing one afternoon, and her Mom was listening to us sing from just outside the room.

After we had been worshiping for some time, she came into the room and told us our worship was so powerful, she felt God's presence so strongly in the living room, that at one point she couldn't enter.

She stayed back in the kitchen where she was and prayed. Then she believed the Lord wanted her to come tell us that we weren't to wait for a perfected song, but we were to go out and sing and play music for Him.

This seemed a bit scary to us. None of us felt we were ready as a band yet. We didn't know where to begin, and we were actually just having fun worshiping God and singing our songs privately without any real "plan" to do much more.

The thing that propelled us into action was the little seeds of faith we each had. We believed God had brought us together and that this mom was speaking God's will to us. That simple seed of faith propelled us into a season where we began playing music at several local churches, ministering to people, and encouraging the local church in ways seen and unseen.

Reading Romans today, faith can mean many different things depending on the context of the scripture. It can mean faithfulness. It can mean trust. But one thing that it never means: a deed I can work up on my own. Faith is a gift given to us from God.

Often times we don't make any effort to reach out beyond ourselves, but I know firsthand what a blessing it is when we do. People often leave it to the pastor and his wife, or the schoolteacher, or the politicians to make things happen. The end result is burnt-out leadership in our schools, churches, and communities. If every person spent a little more time using their talents to bless others in their churches, schools and communities (even just a once-a-year offering), imagine how this could bring about change?

If you are spending more time feeling depressed about your sorrows, and you are not using any of your abilities to bless others or to reach out, you will only find yourself more depressed and deeper in darkness. Let this time in prayer and in God's word transform how you *act* and determine what actions you will take.

If the door is closed at your church for you to offer a blessing to them (this happens more often than I think it should) then find another place where you can use your gifts to shine God's light. I have been amazed at how God has closed doors to me at times within my own church. But it has led me to another open door because God wanted to use me to reach beyond my known sphere of influence.

Yes, it may be frightening to take a step. But the adventure awaits you. The abundant life you were meant to live begins with you having the courage to take that first step. Then the next. And the next. Pray first, then move each time God says to move.

Challenge 10 is to inspire you. Consider this your official "kick in the booty."

10 Action Challenges

Flex Your Faith Muscles

Ideas. Ideas. Ideas. They are endless. So climb in your Daddy's lap today and ask Him, "Hey, Dad. What do you want to do today?"

JOURNAL

Take a moment to write down the ideas as they come to you.

The following ideas just scrape the surface of endless possibilities. Think way outside these perimeters, go beyond the suggestions! Have fun with this and most importantly, make it happen already!

This challenge is not for everyone!

I feel it is important to clarify that these challenges are not necessarily for everyone. They are not meant to overwhelm or cause anxiety. Nor should they distract a person from the course they are on if that course is one God has set a person on. Some of you are already extremely active in your church and community. Some of you are wearing multiple hats: mom, employee, teacher, cook, house cleaner, gardener, family chauffeur—the list goes on.

This list of ideas might cause you to think, "I should be doing this!" when really, you shouldn't.

That is the kind of person I am, so I understand. We are the ones who need to STOP. Sit down. Listen to Jesus. Breathe. He does not want us to be anxious or too busy. That's a way our enemy uses to distract us and overwhelm us, so he can keep us from getting our daily orders from God.

I encourage you to read these challenges and prayerfully ask God if He wants you to take action. But do NOT decide on your own to do one little thing! Doing a work that God is not calling you to do is futile, a work that will burn and not last eternally.

Prayerfully Take the Challenge
The #1 thing to remember: Take everything to prayer before acting.

You might have had a tragedy happen in your life, and you might still be in a stage of grief. Serving others could be just the thing to help you rediscover the joy that comes through giving.

You might be complaining, "My church doesn't have …." Or "our community needs…" Such and such…whatever it may be.   Guess what? YOU are the church. YOU are the community. If you want it to happen:

1. Pray and ask God if He wants it to happen (He might not for His own reasons).

2. Take a step of faith and go to your pastor or leader; let them know your idea and that you are willing to help make it happen, or be a part of a solution to see it come about. Your pastor is not called to make every idea the people have happen. That would be humanly impossible, and pastors and leaders are not Divine and cannot do all things. I've been married to one for nineteen years; I ought to know.

3. Your pastor or leader may say, "Go for it," or they may not. If not, God may be using them to tell you, "Not My will," or "Bad timing," or "Ask again." Do not be discouraged or bitter toward your leader if that happens. That will only reveal to them a selfish and immature attitude, and they will be glad they did not entrust you with something. Rather, let a rejection springboard you into prayer. Ask God to show you if His desire might be to do something else through you.

4. Some of these ideas you can do on your own without the blessing of community leaders or church leaders. But most things are going to require you to reach out and work with people because none of us are meant to be an island. God intends us to be connected to others. That's where the real growth comes. That is why being a committed member of a Bible-teaching church is crucial to your health as a follower of Christ.

Love Kids?

The ideas of how you can make a difference are endless here. Not enough people in this world appreciate the joy which children bring. Not enough people want to take the time to hang out with kids and teach them about God's love. If you happen to be someone who loves kids, you could make a killer impact on your church and community by simply carving out a couple of hours a week to hang with the little ones. Of course you can't be all things to all people, and the need will be very great. Pick one thing and get really great at it.

LOVE KIDS ideas to springboard from:

*Organize occasional kids' nights at your church, allowing parents to go out on a date night.
*Offer to watch kids for a couple who you notice could use a night out.
*Offer to teach a Sunday school class at church once or twice a month.
*Volunteer to read to kids at a bookstore or at the library.

Love Green?

Don't just plant something in your own yard. This time:
*Offer to do something in a friend's garden or for your church.
*Consider starting up a community garden with your church members who have a green thumb and a heart to brighten up the community.

Tim the Tool Man or Woman

Don't just fix up something in your own house, but:
*Offer to help your church or a family in need with a project they need to get done.

Betty Crockers & Chef Boy-R-Dees

*Bring something over to a neighbor's house or offer to take a baked treat to a new family who visited your church.
*Organize a bake sale and use it to raise funds for your next church event. Our ladies have been successful with this one!
*Host a barbecue and cook up something awesome. Our men ROCK at this one!
*Team up with a musician to make a meal at a house concert for the guests while the musician provides the entertainment or leads worship. In fact, call me about that one! I am game!

Renoirs and Van Goghs

*Offer to paint during a church worship service, or offer to paint the set for the next church or school play.
*Offer a free painting class at your church as a community outreach.

Hallmark Poets
*Getting a hand written card is rare these days. If this is something you enjoy doing, bless all kinds of people by reaching out this way. Include Bible verses to encourage those you send cards to.

Freds & Gingers
*Teach a free dance class at your church as a community outreach!
*Choreograph a dance and offer to perform it at your church or at a local event.

Party Planners
*Host a house concert for a local singer/songwriter.
*Get on the church event planning committee and help plan some rockin' events.
*Help plan the next holiday luncheon or tea

Fashionistas
*Plan a special event for your women and ask ladies to model certain outfits, or show off hats or handbags that church members might be trying to sell. Use the event to raise money for an important event.

Hair Stylists & Makeup Artists
*Plan a special event at your church and bless some ladies with a makeover day.

Workout Gurus
*Bless your community and churches by hosting free or inexpensive workshops where they can work out.

Actors, Playwrights, Film Makers:
*Write powerful skits that bring home biblical messages for your church's children's ministry or youth group.
*Act and perform in skits at local outreaches or for fundraisers

Go the extra mile and share your talents and skills with the people within your sphere of influence. There may be someone who needs to hear or see the message you bring in a way that only you can communicate it!

In my town, I know a woman who is the perfect living example of someone who uses everything she has to bless the Lord and directs people to Him in my community. She hosts fundraising events in her home; she wrote a book and gives free copies out to hospitals; she leaves books in hotel rooms. She has experienced loss, discouragement and opposition, but that hasn't stopped my friend Becki Brown from letting her light shine!

Whatever you do, bring your very best! Most importantly, remember it isn't all about you. I have seen some of these very ideas get rained on because of ego. I CHALLENGE you to leave your egos at the door and strive to be a team player.

Our lives *can* be lived out as act of worship to God, and a means of sharing God's redemptive message.

Your life has a purpose. God puts passion in your heart, and He often guides us through our dreams and desires. No, they usually don't happen in our time or according to our plans. However, if we work hard at our God-given talents and choose to be resourceful in faith while waiting in prayer, we will see God work His will out in us and through us.

Do you long to experience life out of the ashes? It all starts by first saying YES to God. Watch God reveal the next chapter of your life. Watch God bring up radiant beauty out of barren ground. Just like the fire lily.

LIFE-MAP PROJECT
"Stones of Remembrance"

For those of you who are interested, this is a fun, if not time-consuming, project. It is NOT a weekly challenge, but something you may work on little by little, or get away and do over a weekend with some friends, much like scrap booking. I am actually still working on mine! There is no rush to get it done, and some of you may not wish to do it at all. That's fine. But if you decide to do it, it will be a treasure you can pass down through generations.

The Life Map idea came to me as I was reading about the stones of remembrance that are mentioned in the Bible. When God brought the Israelites out of Egypt, they would make little rock monuments to remind them of what God did.

READ about the stones of remembrance in Joshua 4:1-9

This challenge is for you to make your own "Stones of Remembrance" of sorts. Draw out a map of your life journey thus far, as a way to visually remember the moments when God worked in a special or powerful way.

I suggest you sketch out the first draft and then re-do it on a poster board, or if you are a serious artist, a canvas. Be as artistic as you like with this.

IDEAS: You could use a timeline. Perhaps you could use a large shoebox and map it out with stick figures and mini-houses. Perhaps you will just use words with cool fonts and pen colors. Or you could do this as a scrapbook, recording a different event on each page.

1. Record your birth date.
2. Record the age when you first realized some of your talent and ability.
3. Record the thing or things that led you to seek after God.
(For example, when I read The Chronicles of Narnia at ten years old, I started to wonder more about God.)
4. Record those moments that have shaped you into who you have become. (Ex: your first love, when you met your closest friends, teachers who impacted you, your first job, your first heart break, engagement and wedding dates, birth of your children, grandchildren, death of a loved one)

Note: Perhaps your past brings back painful, disturbing memories. These do not need to be recorded, unless you feel this was something that led you closer to God. If recording it leads you down a path of dark thoughts, then don't go there.

This is a challenge that should be a positive, fun experience—kind of like scrapbooking—but it takes time! If you do choose to take on this challenge, focus on things that lead you to thoughts that are healthy and positive.

This life map is to help you see the moments when God intervened in your life. A good test to decide what to record is to ask yourself, "Is this something I want my grandchildren to see when I am gone?"
5. In a bold pen color, record the Bible verses that impacted you at different seasons of your life.

6. Most importantly, record the moments where you recognize God was at work:

> Through a circumstance in your life to lead you down a specific path
> By speaking to you through others
> Where He led you through scriptures
> To deliver you from a painful hardship
> To heal you from loss or illness

Be as artistic and creative as you want with this! It will be a wonderful visual for you to reflect on, gain perspective, and see how God has been with you throughout your life. After you have done this, keep this map and add to it as often as you wish. You can use it as a springboard to thank and praise God for all He has brought you through and for what He has in store for your future. At some point, I suggest you laminate it so it will be a keepsake. Pass it on to your children, grandchildren, and beyond. It is a wonderful legacy.

Share Your Testimonies & Life Maps With Me!
We would like to have some examples of Life Map projects to post on the Fire Lilies website, as inspiration for future readers. If you would like to share yours, contact us through the website.

"I'll Remember You"

by Kim Krenik, Staci Frenes

Saw your city streets filled with the hungry and the broken
Alleyways darkened with fears unspoken
Looked into your children's eyes,
Weary from the restless nights
I won't be the same again
Holding one small hand

CHORUS
When the sun goes down here
Rises where you are
I'll remember you
When we lift our eyes up
To the same bright star
I'll remember you

Tucked my babies into bed where they sleep safely and
sound
Gazed out at the moon shadows dancing on the ground
Looked around at all I have
Blessed with more than I could ask
Feeling my heart change
I'll never be the same

BRIDGE
Holding my own child, Fragile, yet strong
Across the world, I know you do the same

Sneak Peak

"The Fire Lilies Testimonies"

A six-week Bible study that includes six powerful stories of resurrected hearts. Here is a teaser from one of the six testimonies in the book.

1

"A Fire Lilies Marriage"

This is a story about our marriage. If you are going through similar pain, we hurt with you. We pray that our story will lead you to a newfound hope.

HE SAID:

    I had a jaundiced view of women. I was raised in a broken home with abuse. My ungodly lifestyle in high school and my experiences fed my addiction to self. Self-protection fueled me in every way. I learned to manipulate others and to gain control of my surroundings as a means of protecting myself.

I didn't understand that I was incapable of truly protecting myself, that I could depend on the Lord to protect and guide me.

My life was built around me. My way, my thoughts, were what mattered. Sadly, my view was that my wife was a nice addition to my life, but she had to revolve around me. My conniving, manipulation, and subtle put-downs eventually eroded even Heather's confidence. I saw Heather through the lens of my own mother, and it colored every single move she made.

To put it plainly, I was a jerk—a first class, self-absorbed ego. Heather never stood a chance. I plucked and picked and harried and harassed the beautiful flower that God planted in my garden until it was the most forlorn Christmas bush on the lot.

SHE SAID:

One day, after we had been married a few years, a woman called me whom I hadn't heard from in a long time. She said she was prompted to call and ask about my marriage. I shut her out, thinking she was being used of the devil to destroy my marriage.

A few years passed, and this same friend sent me a book in the mail called, The Verbally Abusive Relationship. For the first time ever, someone was able to articulate what I had not been able to put my finger on for 10 years. She described my life in detail. Suddenly, my eyes were open.

I did not feel that divorce was an option. I felt that the Lord had me where He wanted me, and that I had to learn to lean on Him alone. I knew that only the Lord could change Scott's heart and heal mine. Even so, if He chose not to, I was determined to shine my light right where He had me.

I began to intentionally practice Peter's counsel in 3:9, "do not return evil for evil or insult for insult, but giving a blessing instead!"

It was not easy, and I fell prey to my flesh time and time again, but the Lord continued to sustain me. He gave me peace and joy, though mingled with tremendous sorrow. I struggled down this path for another 9 years.

HE SAID:

As the years went on, I was miserable. I could not stand being around Heather, she was a living reminder of what a real relationship with Christ looked like. I resented how inferior that made me feel.

I could not go on much longer, and at one point I asked the Lord to take my life. Heather and the kids had a good life insurance policy and would be taken care of. Since I climbed towers, bridges, and dams for a living, it should be pretty easy to die.

I waited for about 6 months and nothing happened. I began to take chances in an effort to help God along but still nothing happened.

About 3 months before Heather left, I changed my mind and uttered the previously unutterable: "God, do whatever it takes to get me into Heaven." Time seemed to stand still as I waited for an answer.

CHANGE ON THE HORIZON

SHE SAID:

One Sunday afternoon my sister in Virginia called. She spoke to me firmly and with authority, "Heather, I feel like the Lord has a word for you. The word is, 'change.'"

At first, I felt terrified. I knew what that word meant. I could not continue down the path I was on. People were noticing the abuse in my marriage. It was evident in my children as well. It was time for change, and I needed to take action and leave.

Suddenly, an inexpressible feeling came over me. I had never experienced anything like it before. Complete euphoria... the exquisite sensation of *freedom!* ...Unthinkable.... Unimaginable. As quickly as it came, it left as I slammed the door shut on the elated feeling and responded dully, "Not possible." Then I stopped and realized I needed to pray.

Ten minutes later, my mom, who lives in Idaho, called and had the same word to share with me.

"Have you been talking to Julie?" I asked. My mom said she hadn't talked to my sister in weeks. After this conversation, I was shaken to the core. None of my family members knew the extent of my situation as I had refrained from sharing too much. But they were not ignorant. They had also experienced their own personal rejection and isolation from Scott, in spite of their attempts to extend a hand of friendship, love, and kindness.

Could this be the Lord? This certainly was not what I had in mind. I needed to be certain of something this serious. I asked, "Lord, if this is you, I need confirmation by at least 3 other people who know nothing of my situation. And... where will I go? My family is dispersed throughout the states, and I don't want to be a burden to anyone."

In a day, I had more than three confirmations from different people, and I had a temporary place to stay. It astonished everyone who saw it unfold. It was completely beyond the realm of possibility.

The Lord was moving swiftly. Scott was gone on business and would return in 4 days. I left while he was away. When he came home, the kids and I, along with our clothes and personal belongings, were gone. Left behind was a note that said my lawyer would be contacting him.

It was a messy situation, and half of me died that week as I wrestled with the loss of a marriage, its impact on my 10 and 11 year-olds, my friends, my church, my family, my testimony, etc. All I can say is the Lord parted waters in amazing ways as I took each step in faith, one stumbling limp at a time.

HE SAID:

It happened while I was climbing and inspecting a tower in Alaska. I had climbed all week in the bitter cold and was excited to get home. When I touched down in Seattle on Thursday night, I had the cold walls of our empty house and the whining of our dog as a shocking welcome home. Heather was gone, she would not say where, but that I could see the kids that Sunday if I wanted.

It was nearly instantaneous that the Holy Spirit convicted me that the trouble was entirely mine. I tried to keep a brave face with my 10 and 11 year-olds that Sunday, but nothing could stop the tears.

The heated whirlwind of the Holy Spirit was just beginning. Monday morning, two guys from the church showed up to discuss Heather's parenting plan, child support, and what weekends I could see the kids. We discussed Heather's plan to sell and divide the company, the house, our property, and vehicles.

FIND OUT HOW THIS COUPLE'S true story progresses and turns out, and discover other stories of resurrected hearts in "The Fire Lilies Testimonies." It includes Bible study questions and challenges in every chapter.

Visit www.kimkrenik.com if you would like to inquire about having Kim as a guest worship leader or a musical guest at your church, retreat or event. She is also available for House Concerts/Nights of Worship.

Did you know?
House Concerts and Retreats are a fun time to gather your study groups and bring out all your Life Maps (works in progress). It is also a great way to share your faith with friends and relatives.

Connect with Kim on any of these social media platforms:

www.kimkrenik.com
www.facebook.com/kimkrenikmusic
www.twitter.com/kimkrenik
www.pinterest.com/kimkrenik
www.instagram.com/dreamersinger

Find encouragement, bible study tools, songs and stories of inspiration at www.firelilies.com

"Of making books there is no end, and much study wearies the body. Now all has been heard; here is the conclusion of the matter:
Fear God and keep his commandments, for this is the whole duty of man. For God will bring every good deed into judgment, including every hidden thing, whether it is good or evil."

Ecclesiastes 12:12-14

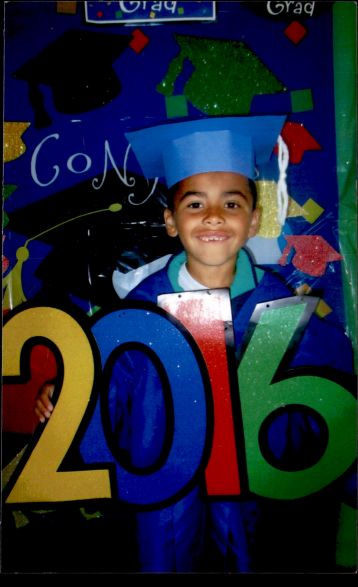

Made in the USA
San Bernardino, CA
12 July 2016